I0828261

Academic Culture
in the
Spanish Colonies

Academic Culture in the Spanish Colonies

BY

JOHN TATE LANNING
Associate Professor of History in Duke University
Managing Editor of
The Hispanic American Historical Review

OXFORD UNIVERSITY PRESS
LONDON NEW YORK TORONTO
1940

Second Printing, 1941

PRINTED IN THE UNITED STATES OF AMERICA BY
THE SEEMAN PRINTERY, INC., DURHAM, N. C.

These essays are adapted from lectures first delivered in January, 1939, before the Winter Institute of Hispanic-American Studies of the University of Miami

Preface

THESE PRELIMINARY essays are the by-products of long investigation of the universities of Spain in America. As now outlined and written, this larger work on the Colonial Universities of Hispanic America will embrace (1) the establishment of universities in the Indies, (2) academic administration, (3) university life, (4) the teaching of the native languages, (5) language and literature in the universities, (6) scholastic philosophy and the decline of authority, (7) Hippocratic medicine and its modernization, (8) the evolution of general science, (9) the reforms of Charles III, and (10) the lessons of the education of the generation of 1810. To make matters worse, more often than not it was necessary to undertake the monographs before grappling with the syntheses. Naturally, then, in the last few years the undertaking has reached cumbersome two-volume proportions. Meanwhile, the uninterrupted fortunes of war have constantly prevented the final check upon papers in the Archives of the Indies in Seville. To proceed without this precaution would be unsound. Therefore, while the essays here published only touch lightly upon four of the ten subjects treated extensively in the major work, they will convey some idea of the extent of the material used and the interpretation put upon it before an irrevocable commitment is made in complete publication. This explanation is presented in the hope that so small a book upon so large a subject will not be denied *ad interim* status.

These summaries were first written in the form of lectures delivered in January, 1939, before the Winter Institute of Hispanic-American Studies of the University of Miami. "The Last Stand of the Schoolmen" was read—essentially as it appears here—at the December, 1938, meeting of the American Historical Association in Chicago. No formal bibliography is offered, because an extensive one will soon be published and because all pertinent data are submitted in the first citation in the notes. Apologies for eighteenth-century Latin texts, which, for example, have *operamdum* for *operandum* and *persuacerit* for *persuaserit*, do not seem sufficiently necessary to warrant the customary *sic*.

The prolonged travel and voluminous copy work upon which the ultimate study is based were made possible by the John Simon Guggenheim Memorial Foundation, the American Council of Learned Societies, and the Duke University Research Council. At the proper time acknowledgment of a vast indebtedness to an almost equally vast list of men will be made.

JOHN TATE LANNING

Duke University
March 24, 1940

Contents

UNIVERSITIES

CHAPTER I

THE TRANSPLANTATION OF THE SCHOLASTIC UNIVERSITY

I

FOUR hundred and two years ago (1538), and within less than a half-century after the discovery of America, a university for the New World was sanctioned. Eight others were actually opened before even a college was established in English America. So thorough, in fact, were the Spaniards in transferring their institutions that they not only gave America its closest approximation to the European universities but necessarily superimposed upon them much of their Old-World dross.

These institutions, established in a strictly medieval society, had been functioning from fifty years to three centuries in Spain before the Indies were graced by one of them. The University of Palencia, appearing near the beginning of the thirteenth century, for some time served as a model in the Iberian peninsula. There alone universities were founded by royal decree before 1350. But the methods of creating Palencia, Salamanca, and their medieval successors, are not to be separated too widely from the system of gradual growth which characterized universities elsewhere.[1]

[1] Cf. Charles H. Haskins, *The Rise of Universities* (New York, 1923), *passim*. A university is here understood to be an institution

Palencia suffered many vicissitudes and early extinction, but not before it had made signal contributions to university history. There it was that the founder and benefactor of the institution, Alfonso VIII of Castile, established endowed professorships and invited teachers from Paris and Bologna to assume chairs. Such favorable commentaries upon the intellectual life of Spain and such indications of the influence of non-Iberian models and centers of study built a noble tradition for Salamanca. The alleged transfer of the university at Palencia to the traditional center of Spanish higher education[2]—sometimes said to have taken place in 1246—could not have been so significant.

Started some time before 1230, Salamanca was refounded in 1242 by Ferdinand III, a man conspicuously associated with the rise of Spanish universities. Through the timely efforts of Alfonso X (the Learned)[3] it was saved the repeated oscillations of fortune and ultimate extinction suffered by Palencia. Himself illustrious as a poet and lawgiver, Alfonso was worthy of the significant rôle he played as patron of so distinguished a school. Having its undisputed inception as a university in the charter granted by Alfonso the Learned in 1254,[4] Salamanca si-

---

organized to teach and to pursue the study of the higher branches of learning and empowered by the king and pope (usually both) to confer degrees in approved fields, as arts, theology, law and medicine.

[2] An example is Luis Paz, *La Universidad Mayor, Real, y Pontificia de San Francisco Xavier de la capital de los Charcas* (Sucre, 1914), p. 108.

[3] Alfonso el Sabio, 1252-1284.

[4] For general information on this stage of the Spanish univer-

multaneously came into the possession of the exemptions and privileges which made the Spanish university almost an *imperium in imperio* before the idea got abroad that royal sanction for a university was necessary. Thus privileges later considered inimical to the royal authority and the dignity of the royal officers, such as the special university courts and the arming of the rector's lackeys, came to secure royal confirmation.

In 1255 Salamanca was raised to the enviable position of one of the four *studia generalia* alongside Paris, Bologna, and Oxford,[5] where degrees were recognized and to which students were supposed to come from all Europe. Despite the royal character of the university's creation, it is not surprising that it remained essentially a cathedral school under the direction of the *Magister Scholarum* who conferred degrees at night in the hushed awe of the cathedral nave. The *Scholasticus* or *Magister Scholarum*, invested by Alfonso the Learned with the power to imprison or to banish scholars, became in America the strong ceremonial office of *Maestrescuela*.

Many of the anachronistic peculiarities of the Spanish colonial universities date naturally from this epoch. The right of the scholars to obtain absolution

sities, see Hastings Rashdall, *The Universities of Europe in the Middle Ages* (2 vols., Oxford, 1895), II, part I, pp. 66, 68, 69; part II, p. 70; Vicente de la Fuente, *Historia de las universidades, colegios y demás establecimientos de enseñanza en España* (4 vols., Madrid, 1884-1889), I, *passim*.

[5] J. de D. Méndez y Mendoza, *Historia de la Universidad Central de Venezuela* (2 vols., Caracas, 1911-1924), I, 13.

for assaults on the masters and clerks is one of many testimonies of the importance of students in the Spanish university, and an indication that the academic life of the middle ages was perhaps more democratic than at the present time. The right of Salamanca's graduates to teach in all the *studia generalia* except those of Paris and Bologna illustrates the curious way in which the Spaniards, both at home and in America, sought to dignify their universities by establishing their station and prestige through law and decree.[6]

The very word *claustro* (the English cloister) is redolent of ecclesiastical associations and its use in Spanish to designate the corporate academic community testifies to the ancient connection between the Spanish universities and cathedrals. In keeping with this association two conservators, the dean of Salamanca and another ecclesiastic, took charge of lodging and other student affairs usually entrusted to a committee of laymen and students.

The legislation of the great scholar-kings, Ferdinand III and Alfonso X, is the basis of the organization of the colonial universities of Spanish America. It was in 1263 that the widely heralded code, *Las Siete Partidas,* a section of which was devoted entirely to universities of the kingdom, was

[6] In the Spanish-American universities degrees continued to be conferred in the name of both king and pope. See *Constituciones, y ordenanzas antiguas, añadidas, y modernas de la Real Universidad, y Estudio General de San Marcos de la Ciudad de los Reyes del Perú* (Lima, 1735), tít. II, const. 28. Rashdall, *op. cit.*, II, part I, p. 72.

issued by Alfonso the Learned.[7] In Spain it constituted the general law of public instruction in the universities of the thirteenth and fourteenth centuries.[8] It has been recognized as the first code of higher education in Europe.

The first law quaintly asserts that the university should be in a region "of good air, in a villa of beautiful portals . . ., because the masters who demonstrate knowledge and the scholars who learn should live well in them and enjoy themselves and find pleasure in the evening when they have tired themselves with study." One requisite in the eyes of the wise king was a city abundant and cheap both in provisions and lodgings. Another was a neighborhood where the citizens would respect and honor the professors and the students—an indication that the characteristic town-and-gown antipathies were not long in appearing. As if such provisions were not minute enough to promote the happiness of the university, a general law of immunities was accorded to the students of Salamanca. And the professors, be it ever said in recognition of the foresight of Alfonso the Learned, were gravely admonished not to interrupt one another unduly.[9] There were few counterbalancing restrictions upon the scholars. Gratuitous advice given the students, however, indicates that they then shared many things with those of the

[7] *Las Siete Partidas*, part. II, tít. xxxi, leyes 1-11; part. I, tít. iv, ley 7. This code remained the guiding spirit of the Spanish university until the reforms of Charles III.

[8] *Ibid.*, tít. xxxi.

[9] *Ibid.*, leyes 2 and 5.

colonies and those of today. They were not to raise bands nor to fight the townspeople where they resided. Instead of prowling at night and annoying their neighbors, they were adjured to "remain calmly in their lodgings . . . to study, to learn, and to formulate a good honest life." With these ends in view students and masters were expected to elect a rector whom they would all obey.

The obligations of this official, in addition to executive duties peculiarly modern, would certainly astonish a university president today. The rector's duties were to suppress not alone the feuds and quarrels arising among the scholars but those between the students and the townspeople; to enforce the fundamental but much neglected rule of the medieval universities that students should not walk abroad at night nor bear arms. And, in fact, the rector was endowed with the authority to punish all offenses and crimes—violations of oaths, constitutions, and other transgressions—except those which involved mutilation or capital punishment. These, as well as lesser crimes with which the rector failed to deal, fell within the jurisdiction of the king's judges. In civil cases an offending student was allowed to appear before either the bishop or his own teacher.[10]

The university of the middle ages, like the political theory of that epoch, was rather universal than national in character. In consequence the age required special protection for students travelling to

[10] *Las Siete Partidas,* part. II, tít. xxxi, ley 7.

and from the Spanish university, especially those from foreign countries. The requirement that students were not to be arrested for the debts of their kinsmen or countrymen is an indication that the temptation to mete out a vicarious justice was sometimes irresistible.

Owing to the circumstances of the origin of the Spanish university, learned men enjoyed an advantageous position in society which remained in full force during the colonial period and still survives in considerable vigor in most places in the Spanish world. Masters of laws were extended privileges which indicate both the prestige of a professorship and the dignified place occupied by law in the curriculum of Salamanca. It was openly declared that the science of laws was the fountain of justice, a science from which the world profited more than by any other. Masters of civil laws were called "*Caballeros*" or "*Señores de Leyes*." Upon the entrance of a doctor of civil laws into the court room, the judge was required to arise and offer him a seat on the bench. More important still, the doctors of law were accorded the privilege of constant access to the person of the king, a favor sometimes denied courtiers. And after twenty years, upon superannuation,[11] they were to be created counts and provided for in the most handsome and honorable manner.[12]

The legislation of Alfonso the Learned was the first authoritative attempt to define the *studia gene-*

[11] *Jubilación* in America.

[12] *Las Siete Partidas*, part. II, tít. xxxi, leyes 2 and 8.

ralia anywhere in Europe. *Studia,* Alfonso laid it down, are of two kinds, general and private. The general, established either by the pope or emperor, should embrace such fundamental chairs as grammar, logic, rhetoric, arithmetic, geometry, astrology, and civil and canon law. The monarch who, in the rôle of philosopher-king, was to keep in mind the skill of the professor and the value of the subject taught, was entrusted with the duty of fixing the professorial salaries. The scale was so graded that the master of laws received just twice as much as the bachelor in the same subject.

This royal function of defining the curriculum was an exaltation of the lay authority, but the jurists held that the *studium generale (respectu regni)* so constituted did not confer degrees of ecumenical value. While two centuries later under the royal patronage it became the custom of the Spanish kings alone to establish the prestige and relative value of the American degrees, universal validity for those of Spain had to be acquired by imperial decree, papal bull, and long usage; the Spanish ones were not regarded as having acquired such distinction merely by custom *(jus ubique docendi).*[13]

The imitators of Salamanca continued to preserve the prestige of law, but with the later development of theology in the Spanish institutions, this branch of learning took the prime position throughout the colonial epoch. The popes, however, were eager to preserve the monopoly of theological Paris.[14] And,

[13] *Ibid.*, part. II, tít. xxxi, leyes 1 and 3.

[14] Rashdall, *op. cit.*, II, part II, p. 75.

while the civil and canon law made Salamanca famous, no theological doctors made their appearance there before 1315. Pedro de Luna, the Avignon candidate for the papacy, intervened at Salamanca and, upon becoming Pope Benedict XIII, instituted reforms which created theological chairs in Salamanca that were endowed by kings John I and Henry III;[15] but Salamanca's interest in theology still remained contingent upon its interest in Paris. It was not until after the encouragement of Martin V (1417-1431), who shared a widespread antagonism for Paris, that the popes came to turn more and more to Salamanca. The impetus which he gave the school of theology at Salamanca made it little less than the oracle of Catholic Europe.

Simultaneously with the development of Spain as the leading empire of the world, Salamanca surpassed the universities of Europe with its four thousand students and a community of seven thousand. The university in general thus acquired a prestige that operated strongly in favor of the Americas petitioning for such institutions. In the course of the centuries traditions were piled up at Salamanca upon the foundations laid by Alfonso the Learned until the reputation of the masters, the solemnity and pomp of the public acts, and the renown of the men who went out from there made the name of Salamanca celebrated throughout the world.

[15] Fuente, *op. cit.*, I, 208 *et seq.;* H. Denifle, *Die Entstehung der Universitäten des Mittelalters bis 1400* (1 vol., Berlin, 1885), I, 492, cited in Rashdall, *op. cit.*, p. 77. See also pp. 75-77.

Under the guiding hand of Ximénez de Cisneros, the *Siglo de Oro* added the University of Alcalá (1498) as a model institution for America. That Salamanca and Alcalá were upon a pinnacle of glory at the time of the conquest contributed first to the dignity of the American universities and later to their somewhat intransigent character. Other universities of Spain antedating those of the American colonies —Valladolid (1346), Lérida (1300), Huesca (1359), Sigüenza (1489)—were a score or more in number, but they had little or no influence in the Indies and that of Alcalá was not great.

II

The Dominican Order in Santo Domingo in 1538 succeeded in obtaining a papal bull which raised its college to the rank of university or *studium generale*.[16] It is possible that no university began to function in the island until after 1558,[17] when the secular University of Santiago de la Paz or Gorjón was approved. There can be no admissible doubt however, about the quiet arrogation of degree-confer-

[16] Despite the vehement controversy on every hand, the documentation from many unrelated sources in the first part of the eighteenth century is based upon the assumption or common knowledge of the existence of the Dominican university. Archivo General de la Nación ([Mexicana], hereinafter cited AGN), *Libro de Gobierno, desde 1737 hasta 1744*; Archivo Histórico de Madrid (hereinafter AH), *Colección de Reales Cédulas*, II, No. 33; Francisco Xavier Hernáez, *Colección de bulas, breves, y otros documentos relativos á la iglesia de América y Filipinas* (2 vols., Brussels, 1879), II, 438-439.

[17] This suggestion is made by Max Henríquez Ureña, *El retorno de los galeones* (Madrid, 1930), p. 90.

ring functions by the Dominicans long before the royal *cédula* arrived which created the Royal and Pontifical University of St. Thomas Aquinas in the eighteenth century.[18]

[18] Fray Cipriano de Utrera, *Universidades de Santiago de la Paz y de Santo Tomás de Aquino y Seminario Conciliar de la Ciudad de Santo Domingo de la Isla Española* (Santo Domingo, 1932), contends that the text (original unfound) of the bull, *In apostulatus culmine*, refers to things which did not exist and that the chapter of the Dominican Order of Salamanca, 1551, notwithstanding its detailed discussion of the work of the order in Santo Domingo, did not mention such a university or its bull of foundation.

Confusion alone has reigned over the subject of universities in Española. The facts seem to be that the bull of 1538, if it is genuine, did not get the approval of the Council of the Indies, which was necessary for the operation of pontifical decrees in the Americas. Certainly when the agents of Hernando Gorjón petitioned the crown some twenty years later for the establishment of a university in the island, they acted upon the assumption that none existed there. The Royal *cédula* of 23 February, 1558, which created the University of Santiago de la Paz or Gorjón under the aegis of the secular *cabildo* (after 1602, Conciliar Seminary), expressed the desire of the government to have "a university" in Santo Domingo. (When the cloister of the University of St. Jerome in Havana after 1728 began its search for the statutes of the University of St. Thomas Aquinas, none could be found. Evidently the Dominicans had run their institution for over a hundred years through the constitutions of Alcalá and some supplementary rules of their own.)

The Jesuits had not long been in the island until they were holding their *Sabatinas* in the decadent Conciliar Seminary and praying the crown to allow them to assume the functions of the institution. Their college had been established since 26 September, 1701, but their petition to supersede the Seminary was not granted until 1745. Thereupon, the Dominicans entered into litigation against the Society with such abandon that it must be assumed that they thought themselves the proper directors of the university by right of preëmption. The issue was the royal decree of 17 February, 1747, approving two universities, one for the Dominicans and one for the Jesuits. Thus the Dominicans at last (26 May, 1757) could bestow upon their institution the title long associated with them: Royal and Pontifical University of St.

With a solemn declaration that their motives were "to honor and favor our Indies and to dissipate the clouds of ignorance," Charles V and the queen-mother in 1551 authorized the two pioneer American universities by declaring that "we create, found and constitute in the City of Lima of the Kingdoms of Peru, and in the City of Mexico of New Spain, schools and universities" with the privileges, exemptions, and limitations of the University of Salamanca.[19] The Royal and Pontifical University of Mexico became, however, the first active major university in the New World upon the inauguration of its courses in 1553,[20] antedating the opening of San Marcos de Lima by approximately twenty-three

Thomas Aquinas. By 1748 the Jesuits had completely taken over the Gorjón institution, or Conciliar Seminary, with the old title of University of Santiago de la Paz. Litigation between the two orders, it is useless to say, continued. So late as 2 August, 1758, a *cédula* was issued, at the behest of the Jesuits and in the interest of the universities of Mexico and San Marcos, denying the Dominicans the use of the word *primacy* in the title of their university (*ibid.*, pp. 173, 218, 225, 248, 252-258, 259, 267).

[19] AGN, *Libro de las Cédulas y Provisiones Reales y Autos del Real Acuerdo*, No. 2, Real cédula, Toro, 21 de septiembre de 1551. Although this document of the Mexican archives makes no reference to Lima, the language above appears in the laws of the Indies (*Recopilación de Leyes de los Reinos de las Indias* [4 vols., Madrid, 1756], lib. I, tít. xxii, ley 1); however, the question arises as to whether or not the juxtaposition was not made in the first or second editions of the *Recopilación.* The problem can be solved easiest through the discovery of the allied documents in Lima, as it appears that the cédula creating the university in Lima was dated 12 May, 1551, and not simultaneously with Mexico. Such disclosures are unlikely in view of the disappearance of the *Archivo* of San Marcos.

[20] AGN, Cristóbal Bernardo Plaza y Jaén, *Crónica de la Insigne y Real Universidad de la Ciudad de México*, lib. I, caps. 1 and 12.

years. Founded fifty-six years before Jamestown and eighty-five years before Harvard, the University of Mexico, and finally its sister institution, became the models for most of the Spanish-American universities to follow, much as Paris had been for Europe and Salamanca for Spain.

As great as is the uncertainty about many phases of the early history of higher education in Spanish America, it is known that both the Mexicans and Peruvians had considered the necessity of such an institution at length and had made formal requests of the king. Although Bartolomé de las Casas apparently did not obtain an order for Viceroy Antonio de Mendoza to establish a university, as Herrera alleged,[21] there was, none the less, a growing sentiment for the establishment of a complete educational hierarchy. The arduous nature of travel imposed upon the young creoles—ambitious and by now wealthy enough to fulfill the hope of a literary or professional career—the mortifying necessity of risking life itself in pursuit of the literary career at Salamanca or Alcalá. And Viceroy Antonio Mendoza was so eager to Hispanize the natives and to bring the educational amenities to the viceroyalty that he made a donation of some cattle ranches to the proposed university as a symbol of his hope and faith, a gift which was finally incorporated as a part of the endowment. But meanwhile he could

[21] Antonio de Herrera, *Historia General de los Hechos de los Castellanos en las Islas i Tierra Firme del Mar Oceano* . . . (4 vols., Madrid, 1601), déc. 6, lib. 7, cap. 6.

only appoint masters to give lessons in the subjects[22] they most esteemed and to lead the people to believe that there would soon be a university with all the requisite chairs. His anxiety dovetailed nicely with the desires of the town council and the ecclesiastical organization. Around 1545 he requested the government to found in New Spain a university, with the "corresponding endowment," of "all the sciences" where both natives and creoles could orient themselves in "the things of our holy Catholic faith and in the remaining faculties."[23] Mendoza was not, however, to open the University of Mexico.

The very administrative vigor of which his promotion of a university was but one phase led to his appointment as viceroy of the turbulent Peru before he had the satisfaction of seeing his project realized. It was during the incumbency of Luis de Velasco that the "very noble and loyal City of Mexico" became the seat of a university with a standing order for a thousand pesos gold from the royal treasury each year.[24] In this charter the faculties of the Mexi-

[22] No names of professors, materials taught, or indication of place or time in which the lessons were given have ever been discovered. The principal support for this position is the known disposition of the first viceroy of New Spain. See J. García Icazbalceta, *Obras* (10 vols., 1896-1899), (second edition, 1905) I, 335-354.

[23] AGN, *Libro de Cédulas y Provisiones* . . ., Real cédula, El Toro, 21 de septiembre de 1551; Real cédula, El Pardo, 4 de octubre de 1560.

[24] Some editors have had Herrera, *op. cit.*, déc. 8, lib. 7, cap. 13, say 100,000 pesos, but the first edition (1615) mentions only one thousand, a sum sustained by the original records. AGN, *Libro de Cédulas y Provisiones* . . ., No. 3; Plaza y Jaén, *op. cit.*, lib. I, cap. 1.

can university had been given all the franchises and privileges of the academicians of Spain. Mexicans were placed on an equal footing with Spaniards and the statutes and royal *cédulas* of Salamanca became the law whereby the University of Mexico was at first governed.[25]

The university was opened with the pomp and solemnity so much the warp and woof of colonial society. The people of New Spain were keenly alive to the significance of the event. Beginning on January 21, 1553, Viceroy Luis de Velasco, attended by the *audiencia*, the tribunals, the religious, and the entire body of men of letters in the kingdom convened on the day of the conversion of St. Paul in the Church of San Pablo[26] where a solemn mass was sung. Emerging from the church, the procession bent its way to the houses of Doña Catarina de Montejo, which Velasco had selected as the site of the university. Each professor was to begin "reading" his course at a separate time to enable the viceroy to honor every opening session with his own presence as well as with that of the *audiencia*.

The first patrons of the New-World institution were naturally the kings of Spain whom the good American scholastics likened unto the fathers who protect the children from danger and engage their loyalty—a symbol of political theory then enjoying

[25] In 1555 the title, "pontifical," was confirmed. AGN, *Libro de Cédulas y Provisiones . . .*, Real cédula dada en Madrid, 17 de octubre de 1572.

[26] There is some question about this location.

a wide vogue. In Mexico and elsewhere patron saints were also selected, sometimes by lot.

If we look for a modern university with experimentation, observation, and skeptical philosophy in 1553, we look in vain. The "seven columns" of learning in the Mexican university, the seven academic chairs, were theology, scripture, canons, arts (logic, metaphysics, physics), laws, decretals, and rhetoric—all upon a base of Latin language. They were to be filled by the viceroy and the *audiencia* in conformity with the prerogatives conferred upon them by Charles V.[27] So far was the Salamancan tradition of legal supremacy now left behind that the ranking chair created was scholastic theology, designed to teach and to defend the sane and secure doctrines of the Holy Fathers, "to impugn, to destroy, to vanquish, and to extirpate that which does not conform to the faith." Some of the occupants of these early chairs held the highest degrees from the Spanish universities and some, in addition, had studied under such intellectual lights of the *Siglo de Oro* as Domingo de Soto.[28] Professors not holding the proper academic titles for the corresponding chairs in Salamanca were promptly endowed with them by the viceroy, rector, and cloister.

Identically the same interests which produced the University of Mexico were at work in Peru, but the continued uprisings of the Indians and the civil

[27] AGN, *Libro de Cédulas y Provisiones . . .*, Real cédula, Toro, 21 de septiembre de 1551.

[28] AGN, Plaza y Jaén, *op. cit.*, lib. I, caps. 3-10.

wars of the conquistadores postponed the establishment of the *studium generale*. The Dominicans, however, always zealous of the training of their religious and appreciating the need for general and basic instruction in the Indian tongues, became the vanguard of the demand. Fray Tomás de San Martín, first provincial of the Dominican Order in Peru, was charged with the presentation of the Peruvian request. And in company with Licenciate Pedro de Gasca he undertook the dangerous voyage to Spain in 1550.[29] No doubt relieved to escape financial responsibility, Charles V welcomed the promise of the Dominicans to house the university in the Convent of San Rosario, and sanctioned the establishment of a university with the privileges and exemptions of Salamanca.[30] For want of funds beyond the 350 pesos allotted, but unpaid by the Dominicans, the project languished. In 1557, the Marqués de Cañete, Viceroy of Peru, designated

[29] Fray Juan Meléndez, *Tesoros Verdaderos de las Indias* (Rome, 1681), pp. 180-181; José Baquíjano y Carillo, "Historia de la fundación, progresos y actual estado de la Real Universidad de San Marcos de Lima," *El Mercurio Peruano*, III (Manuel A. Fuentes edition, Lima, 1861-1864), 221. This monograph was reprinted in the *Anales Universitarios del Perú*, I (Lima, 1862), 1-33, under the editorship of José G. Paz-Soldán.

[30] Biblioteca Nacional de Lima (hereinafter BNL), MSS., *Documentos del Virreinato*, VII: Cédula Real del Señor Emperador Carlos y la Reyna Juana su Madre, sobre la fundación de esta Real Universidad. Valladolid, 12 de mayo de 1551. This date rests upon the authority of Baquíjano (*loc. cit., III*, 221), who had access to the *Archivo* of San Marcos before it was scattered. If correct, the *cédula* of foundation of San Marcos antedated that of Mexico by four months, although no doubt both were the result of the general decision of the Spanish government to sanction universities in America.

the insufficient sum of four hundred pesos for this purpose. It was a generation from the *cédula* of foundation before a papal bull (1571) of confirmation produced symptoms of new life.[31]

In 1571 Philip II ordered the rectorship of the Dominicans suspended and decreed the creation of a cloister of secular doctors. This was the epoch when the University of San Marcos unmistakably arrived. Francisco Teledo now turned energetically to its support, creating an endowment in *encomiendas* of 20,312 pesos.[32] The fear of the Dominicans which was felt by Philip II must have been bolstered by a slight anti-clerical feeling in Toledo. At any rate, the first rector, after the removal of the unborn institution from the Convent of San Rosario, was Gaspar Meneses, a medical doctor; and this despite the fact that medical men came to be barred from this dignity in the constitutions. Upon his death in 1573, he was followed by another physician, the *protomédico* Antonio Sánchez Renedo. The medical doctor, however, recognized the interest of the Dominicans in the institution by making it possible for them to secure degrees by payment of one third of the customary fees.[33]

[31] BNL, MSS., Bulla de Nuestro Muy S. P. Pio, Papa V, 25 de julio de 1571, *Documentos del Virreinato,* XII; Baquíjano y Carillo, *loc. cit.*, III, 222; Meléndez, *op. cit.*, pp. 181-185.

[32] Baquíjano, *loc. cit.*, p. 225.

[33] BNL, MSS., Alonso Eduardo de Salazar y Cevallos, "Razón Histórico-Dedicatoria al Ilustre Claustro de esta Real Universidad . . .," *Documentos del Virreinato,* XII. Archivo de la Universidad de San Marcos, *Libro de Claustros,* No. 1, f. 12, cited by Baquíjano, *loc. cit.*, p. 223.

Under the protection of Toledo striking innovations were effected and new life injected into the moribund institution which had been rescued from the lethargy of the mendicant Dominicans. As a result of the endowment created, Toledo felt free to sponsor the erection of various chairs. In the cloister of September 3, 1576, the doctors created two chairs of *gramática,* one of Indian languages so vital to the propagation of the gospel, three of philosophy, an equal number of theology, three of laws, two in canons, and two in medicine, although only one of these was actually filled. Thus it was not until the year 1578 that the University of San Marcos arrived at the point of development achieved in Mexico in 1553, a retardation due in part to the chaos of the country and in part to the monopoly of the Dominicans. From that time until the period of decadence in the eighteenth century the history of this institution is replete with scholastic achievement and medieval splendor.

Although Mexico and Lima were the model universities in the New World during the colonial period, there were six other institutions which by virtue of having the required five faculties, or by decree, ranked with the former two as major universities. A third class was the minor university. This type of educational institution was largely the work of the Jesuits.

The Counter Reformation reached American intellectual life in two fundamental respects—it imposed the system of orthodoxy devised by the Council of Trent and gave to the New World the Jesuit Society. Specialists in education with an unprecedented reputation abroad, these followers of Ignatius Loyola dominated the sphere of higher education in all but the royal and pontifical universities. None of the religious orders was as well prepared for missionary enterprise and, at the same time, for solid higher education.

The first Jesuits to arrive in Peru in 1569 had hastened to build a church, and at the same time, a college. They anticipated royal authorization, as had the Dominicans before them, in their realization that through the mastery of the native tongues lay the evangelization of the aborigine. Before long, one of the Society, Alfonso Barganza, was proclaiming the gospel in Quechua. Soon a college was founded in Cuzco and another in La Paz,[34] to be followed by a Jesuit house in Potosí in 1577.

The drift was plainly to Los Charcas (later called Upper Peru) as the center of Jesuit spiritual and intellectual domination, for the capital was within reach of a large indigenous population, wrapped in a perennial spring, and conveniently close to the wealth of Potosí. Although José de la Acosta had visited Los Charcas with Toledo in 1573,[35] it was 1592 before the Jesuits arrived in force. These men were preoccupied with immediate problems; but at

[34] J. Crétineau-Joly, *Historia religiosa, política y literaria de la Compañía de Jesús* (3 vols., Barcelona, 1853), cited in Luis Paz, *op. cit.*, p. 25.

[35] A. F. Zimmerman, *Francisco de Toledo, Fifth Viceroy of Peru, 1569-1581* (Caldwell, Idaho, 1938), p. 89.

the end of twelve years, in 1600, the Bishop of Charcas, Alonso Ramírez de Vergara, addressed a letter to the king of Spain emphasizing the necessity of founding a university in the city of La Plata[36] in the very heart of Los Charcas. La Plata, in a fine climate and beautiful valley on the overland route to Buenos Aires, was the resort or retreat for the rich mining families from the altitude and rigors of the famed Potosí. To Bolivians the city has been the "Athens of South America." General Miller, an Englishman, called it the "Oxford of South America."

The Spaniards had some twenty-one universities in the colonial period besides those of Mexico City and Lima. And the refrain of the petition for each one was that the trip to Mexico or Lima was so hazardous and so costly as to stultify youth and stalemate the conferring of degrees. The request of Vergara was, therefore, no exception. Travel from the bishoprics of Tucumán, Chile, and Paraguay to Lima was often out of the question. The eight chairs which he proposed for Los Charcas or Chuquisaca in grammar, rhetoric, theology, arts, and canons, could be supported from the eight thousand pesos rent from two *encomiendas*, a form of wealth so substantial as to be virtually the capital of the colonial epoch. This, with the expected donations from private persons and prelates, would prove sufficient.[37] It was with no sense of the incongruous

[36] City of four names: Los Charcas, La Plata, Chuquisaca, Sucre.

[37] Original in the Archivo General de Indias (hereinafter AGI), cited in Paz, *op. cit.*, pp. 54-55.

that in 1602 Vergara entered another plea for a university which he coupled with a request for a tribunal of the Inquisition, as a necessary complement of the separation of Charcas from Lima. The prestige a most enticing climate had not already supplied was lent the city when, in 1605, an archbishopric was created there. The approval of the *audiencia* made the clamor well nigh universal and the plea more effective. It was the clerical pressure, however, which was first acknowledged. A papal bull of 1621 was followed in the next year by a royal *cédula* of foundation which confirmed the university "for the greater exaltation of the Catholic faith, and the triumph of justice in the New World."[38] The new university was extended the privilege of conferring degrees,[39] and was officially launched with the greatest pomp on April 14, 1624. This university was subjected rigidly to the direction and teaching of the Jesuits until their constitutions and statutes were nullified in the expulsion of the Company, as the Spaniards delighted to call the Jesuit organization. Thereafter the vestiges of the university were conducted through the constitutions of San Marcos de Lima until Charles IV by royal *cédula*[40] (1798) extended to Chuquisaca the statutes, laws, and privileges of the University of Salamanca.

[38] Real cédula de 2 de febrero de 1622.

[39] Archivo Nacional de Bolivia, "Real acuerdo de la audiencia de Charcas, sobre la fundación del colegio y universidad de esta ciudad de 1624," Paz, *op. cit.*, pp. 133-139.

[40] *Ibid.*, pp. 140-141; Real cédula de 10 de abril de 1798.

Although, in general, the Jesuits were expressly forbidden to confer degrees in their colleges,[41] such *cédulas* and briefs as those approving the University of Los Charcas also authorized the colleges of the Society of Jesus in the Philippines, Chile, Tucumán, New Granada, and other provinces to confer the degrees of bachelor, licenciate, doctor, and master where there were no universities within a distance of two hundred miles after the candidates had complied with the customary acts and regulations in the general universities for obtaining degrees.[42]

By the same process universities sprang up elsewhere. Córdoba was fixed upon as a center of Jesuit intellectual activity in the Río de la Plata. Through the energy and last will and testament of a Franciscan friend, Fray Fernando de Trejo, the Society, after a decade of travail,[43] succeeded in having the *Colegio Máximo* elevated to the category of univer-

[41] MSS., *Colección de reales cédulas sobre la Universidad de México*, No. 7: Real cédula dada en el Pardo, 2 de noviembre de 1576.

[42] Alejandro Korn, "Las influencias filosóficas en la evolución nacional," *Revista de la Universidad de Buenos Aires*, Año IX, tomos XVII y XX (1912), p. 463; Pablo Pastells, *Historia de la Compañía de Jesús en la provincia del Paraguay* (Madrid, 1912—), I, 498; Paz, *op. cit.*, p. 113. See Gabriel René-Moreno, *Los últimos días coloniales en el Alto Perú* (2 vols., Santiago de Chile, 1896), I, 25. See also J. V. Jacobsen, S. J., *Educational Foundations of the Jesuits in Sixteenth-Century New Spain* (Berkeley, 1938), pp. 161, 168, 182-184, 198, 205.

[43] J. M. Garro, *Bosquejo histórico de la Universidad de Córdoba* (Buenos Aires, 1882), pp. 17-27; José María Liqueño, *Fray Fernando de Trejo y Sanabria* (2 vols., Córdoba, 1916); Pedro de Lozano, *Historia de la Compañía de Jesús de la provincia del Paraguay* (2 vols., Madrid, 1734-1755), II, lib. xii, caps. 1 and 2; Archivo de la Universidad de Córdoba, *Libros de documentos* (varias materias), *desde 1613 hasta 1798*.

sity by pontifical and royal dispositions in the year 1622.[44] Raised ultimately (1761) to the status of a major university,[45] Córdoba ran a quiet course until the expulsion of the Jesuits who were replaced by the humble followers of St. Francis. The University and the *Colegio Consistorio de Monserrat de Córdoba* were taken away from the Franciscans in 1800 and combined in a royal and pontifical institution with the high-sounding title of *Real Universidad de San Carlos y de Nuestra Señora de Monserrat.*

Although there were some forty colleges and seminaries in Mexico, nineteen of them preparing students to take degrees, the University of Mexico alone carried the title of university, and it alone could confer the coveted titles.[46] On the other hand, the paucity of men of letters, lack of trained priests, and the problems of travel were so great that universities under the sponsorship of local bishops began to secure royal and pontifical confirmation elsewhere in the Spanish colonies. Upon the petition of Bishop Cristóbal de Castilla y Zamora, and between 1680 and 1685, there came into existence, for instance, the Seminary and University of San Cristóbal de Huamanga in Peru, with the privileges and exemptions of the universities of Salamanca and Lima. Although falling upon evil days, its priv-

[44] Archivo de la Universidad de Córdoba, *Libro de Claustros*, No. 1, Real cédula de 2 de febrero de 1622.

[45] Archivo de la Universidad de Córdoba, MSS., Bula y cédula de fundación de la Universidad Mayor de San Carlos, Córdoba, 1761-1778.

[46] AGN, *Substituciones de Cátedras y Lugares, desde 1724 hasta*

ilege of conferring degrees obviated the trip to Lima and satisfied municipal pride.[47]

The ancient renown and importance of Cuzco facilitated the establishment of minor universities there. Students coming from Arequipa, La Paz, and Potosí, gave great prestige to the Dominican Seminary of San Antonio de Abad in Cuzco; but it was the Jesuits, founding the *Colegio Real de San Bernardo,* who forced the establishment of the University of San Ignacio de Loyola in 1628. It was soon conferring all four of the degrees habitual in Spanish institutions. Rivalries between the Jesuit institutions and San Antonio de Abad were natural, for students of the latter had to make the trip to Lima or succumb in a Jesuit examination at home. The furore excited by the situation led to the creation, in 1692, of a second and rival institution called the University of San Antonio de Abad with the power to give degrees.[48] The Jesuits sued to restrain the new university, but their failure was celebrated in a solemn parade to accompaniment of drums, and the notes of trumpets and oboes.

The Dominicans who, as well as the Jesuits, had the privilege of conferring degrees in New Granada,

---

1830. A *colegio* is here understood to be a community of preparatory students, undergraduates, and teachers dedicated to a limited number of subjects as rhetoric, theology, and arts, usually without authority to confer degrees.

[47] Real cédula de Carlos II, 21 de diciembre de 1680, *Anales Universitarios del Perú,* II, 3-4; *ibid.,* p. 7; César Antonio Ugarte, "Las universidades menores," *Revista Universitaria del Cuzco,* Año VI, No. 19, p. 7.

[48] *Ibid.,* pp. 23-28; *Catálogo de reales cédulas* (Matraya), No. 195.

Chile, and the Philippines, when their establishments were two hundred miles distant from Lima or Mexico,[49] also fell into a fierce controversy with their competitors. Their long fight to establish a university in their convent of San Rosario in Bogotá was rewarded by the establishment of a Thomistic University (1594, 1655), while the Jesuits sought the exclusive privilege of conferring degrees in the University of San Francisco de Xavier (Javerians).[50] Their ultimate failure in this undertaking so stimulated their provincial work that upon their expulsion in 1767 they could claim thirteen of the twenty-three educational establishments in the viceroyalty.

The earliest universities of Quito, like those of Bogotá, were mere faculties of the order brought into degree-conferring privileges by special concessions. The University of San Gregorio el Magno, an adjunct of the Jesuit *Colegio Máximo* from 1620, was followed in 1688 by the creation of the Dominican University of Santo Tomás de Aquino which was secularized in 1788.[51] An Augustinian academy, ostentatiously called the University of San Ful-

[49] Alonso Zamora, *Historia de la Provincia de San Antonio del Nuevo Reino de Granada de la Orden de Predicadores* (Barcelona, 1701), pp. 274, 446-459, 465-466; Real cédula, Madrid, 2 de febrero de 1622; *ibid.*, 6 de septiembre de 1624.

[50] See Zamora, *op. cit.*, p. 447; Daniel Restrepo, *El Colegio de San Bartolomé* (Bogotá, 1928), *passim.* The Jesuits were empowered in 1655, at least, to give degrees in their college at Bogotá. The Dominicans enjoyed the privilege of conferring degrees between 1623 and 1633 in their College of Santo Tomás.

[51] *Colección de Bulas, Breves, Cédulas reales y otros documentos relativos a la iglesia de América* (sección: Erección de Universidades). Federico González Suárez, *Historia general de la república del Ecuador* (9 vols., Quito, 1890-1903) VII, 24-25.

gencio, was vested with the faculty to confer doctor's degrees for two hundred years but had so little regard for standards as to confer the doctoral distinction upon a shoemaker of Popayán.[52] San Fulgencio, among the minor universities, is strong documentation for the intellectual barrenness of the seventeenth century in the colonies, so addicted to appearance and pomp.

Similar institutions dotted the perimeter of the Caribbean. Of these, the University of Guatemala had a long and distinguished history. The captaincy-general of Guatemala, completely isolated from Mexico, was sufficiently large to support a university. Its zealous sponsor and benefactor, Father Francisco Marroquín, through his last will and testament,[53] provided the usufruct of so much landed property that scarcely any university in America was as well endowed. It came into its inheritance a century late, for the property was originally devoted to the *Colegio de Santo Tomás de Aquino* of the Dominican Order. It was at first erected upon the foundations of this college and elevated to the rank of Royal and Pontifical University of San Carlos Borromeo de Guatemala in 1681.

A university was established within the College of San Francisco Xavier in Mérida de Yucatán in

[52] Juan de Velasco, *Historia del reino de Quito* (3 vols., Quito, 1841-1844), III, 52; Suárez, *op. cit.*, pp. 26-28; Max Henríquez Ureña, *op. cit.*, pp. 176-177.

[53] Archivo General del Gobierno de Guatemala (hereinafter AGG), Serie A, legajo No. 2, expediente No. 2 (old number). See this document in *Anales de la Sociedad de Geografía e Historia de Guatemala*, tomo XIII, Nos. 1 and 2.

1624. But it was a kind of embellishment of the Jesuit privilege of granting degrees in all places more than two hundred miles from Mexico. Similar complications resulted in the royal *cédula* of 1791 which conceded to Guadalajara its long-sought university.[54] A short time after 1749 there existed a Jesuit university in Panama with authority to confer degrees of bachelor, licenciate and master,[55] while León de Nicaragua was rewarded for long effort with a university in 1815—just on the eve of final separation from the mother country. And after stern opposition from a rival cloister, a university was sanctioned in Mérida, Venezuela, in 1807.[56]

The great outlying captaincies-general of the Spanish empire—Venezuela, Cuba, and Chile—made another step in the ladder of their growing importance by the establishment of universities in all their capitals. By the end of the eighteenth century Caracas, Havana, and Santiago de Chile had each become a seat of higher learning.

After a number of importunities, and at the behest of Bishop Juan José Escalona y Calatayud, a

[54] AGN, *Gobierno de la Universidad de México, desde 1807 hasta 1812*, una carta al rector de la Universidad de México sobre "la Universidad de la ciudad de Mérida, provincia de Yucatan," signed by José Cisneros *et al. Ibid., Reales cédulas*, Vol. 159, f. 47. See also Diego López Cogolludo, *Historia de Yucathan* (Madrid, 1688), pp. 215-216. Manuel Orozco y Berra, *Apéndice al diccionario universal de historia y geografia* (Mexico, 1855-1856), II, 666-668.

[55] Octavio Méndez Pereira, *Historia de la instrucción pública en Panamá* (Panamá, 1916), *passim.* Max Henríquez Ureña, *op. cit.*, p. 193.

[56] Real cédula de 6 de octubre de 1807. The pertinent documents are printed in Méndez y Mendoza, *op. cit.*, I, 175-184.

university of nine chairs, all privately endowed, was raised in 1721-1722 upon the walls of the College of Santa Rosa at Caracas. It was modeled after the University of St. Thomas Aquinas in Santo Domingo.[57] And such a godmother was a proper choice, for, of the ten original members incorporated in the cloister of the University of Caracas with degrees which they then held, seven had acquired all their degrees in the institution of Santo Domingo.[58] The constitutions of the new university, despite its royal as well as pontifical character, indicated a decided trend toward the church. The rector was not only named by the bishop, but two councillors to conserve the principles of the Council of Trent were named to advise him. All, it may be further noted, were required to swear *in licitis et honestis* to abjure and enveigh against the execrable doctrines of tyrannicide and regicide.[59]

Cuba, with nine colleges, three hundred leagues distant from Mexico, had long felt its cultural isolation. An agitation led by the Dominican provincial forced the issue soon after the creation of a univer-

[57] Real cédula sobre la erección del real colegio seminario de la ciudad de Santiago de León de Caracas en universidad real por el Señor D. Felipe V, dada en Lerma á 22 de diciembre de 1721. Méndez y Mendoza, *op. cit.*, I, 24-28. Inscrutabili Divinae Sapientiae atque bonitatis arcano, Bula Apostólica de su Santidad Inocencio XIII por la que se eleva á Universidad pontificia dicha real Universidad (Roma, 18 de diciembre de 1722), *ibid.*, pp. 28-33, 141.

[58] Archivo de la Universidad Central de Venezuela (hereinafter AUC), *Libro de Claustros*, No. 1; Méndez y Mendoza, *op. cit.*, I, 37.

[59] Constitutions confirmed by Real cédula de Felipe V, 8 de mayo de 1727.

sity in Venezuela. Founded upon the chairs of the Dominican Convent of San Juan de Letrán in 1728, it became the Royal and Pontifical University of Saint Jerome. It was modeled also upon the Dominican University of Santo Domingo,[60] but the rector was forced to conform to the privileges and limitations of the University of Alcalá,[61] after which the institution of Santo Domingo was modeled.

In the second decade of the eighteenth century a murmur for a university went up from Santiago de Chile, accompanied with enthusiastic proposals to finance the chairs. When, after a quarter of a century, final pressure was applied at court, a royal concession of 1738 arrived in Santiago for the creation of the University of San Felipe.[62] Although the university, fighting a financial stringency which forced it to sell honorary degrees, was finally founded in 1747, it was a decade in passing over the travail of initiation.[63]

[60] In Havana they had no written records to go on. AH, *Colección de reales cédulas,* III, No. 33. See also Real cédula de Felipe V, Madrid, 23 de septiembre de 1728, "Documentos relacionados con la creación de la Universidad de la Habana," in Juan M. Dihigo y Mestre, *La Universidad de la Habana* (Havana, 1930), pp. 109-135.

[61] Certificación de Joseph Poveda, estatutos, y nombramiento del rector y consiliarios de la Universidad, *ibid.*, p. 122.

[62] This document is printed in the *Anales de la Universidad de Chile,* XLV, 5-8.

[63] For the documentation of the early stages of the University of San Felipe, see Domingo Amunátegui y Solar, *Mayorazgos y títulos de Castilla* (3 vols., Santiago, 1901-1904), III, 244-248; José Toribio de Medina, *Historia de la Real Universidad de San Felipe* (2 vols., Santiago, 1928), I, 1-2, 10-15, 22-23, 35-38, 40, n. 2, 39-44; *ibid.*, II, 8-9; Medina, *Biblioteca hispano-chilena* (3 vols., Santiago, 1897-1899), III, 287-294. Alejandro Fuenzalida, *Historia del desarrollo intelectual en Chile* (Santiago de Chile,

Thus the Spaniards in America founded ten major universities and fifteen minor ones. All the major ones fell into the category of "royal and pontifical" universities; three of them with constitutions modeled strictly upon Salamanca, one upon Alcalá, one upon Mexico, three upon Lima, and two upon Santo Domingo. Of the minor institutions eight were Jesuit, four Dominican, one Augustinian, one Franciscan, and one secular. Thus, omitting two institutions of the post-Jesuit period, there were twenty-three Spanish universities in the New World.[64] A few of them were universities in name only, but it is not enough to say that the others were scholastic and decadent; in reality they were the very warp and woof of the church, without which a trained clergy could not have survived and the very solid rock upon which colonial culture, in all its formal aspects, rested in closest parallel to that of Europe.

1903), pp. 1-7; Archivo Nacional de Chile (hereinafter ANC), *Libro I de Acuerdos de la Universidad de San Felipe*, f. 16.

[61] These totals would not be true of any one year and can be modified by interpretation. Mexico, Lima, and Santo Domingo were "model universities," while Chuquisaca and Córdoba were Jesuit institutions before 1767, and are counted both as minor and major in this summary. Huamanga, although treated as minor by Ugarte, was based upon the statutes of Lima, and is here tentatively classified as major on the grounds of its unique episcopal government. Guadalajara and Nicaragua, for want of satisfactory evidence that they ever functioned as universities, are not counted. By listing the secular and minor University of Mérida de Maracaibo in place of a Jesuit institution of doubtful status, the total remains the same as in the first printing of this book.

Chapter II

UNIVERSITY LIFE AND ADMINISTRATION

I

The constitutions of the American universities,[1] especially in the group modeled after Salamanca, provided that the government should be entrusted to the cloister. This body was composed of the faculty and all the doctors and masters living in or near the university city. Bound by oaths to keep its deliberations secret, it was provided with a privy salon in which the rector, doctors, masters, and councillors were obligated to convene under pain of a drastic fine. In the same room was housed the archive, or registrar's office, accessible only through the use of three keys with each in the hands of a different individual. The general cloister of no less than twenty members was convoked by the *cédula de ante diem* and was denominated "full cloister." The ordinary cloister of no less than ten members met six times a year. A kind of committee of eight on chairs and curriculum, elected by the cloister, was given the name of councillors. The financial committee had the title of council of deputies.[2]

[1] This discussion is based primarily upon the royal and pontifical institutions and unimportant exceptions are ignored.

[2] *Claustro pleno, claustro menor,* and *diputados* were the Spanish names. *Constituciones de la . . . Universidad de México,* tít. IV, constituciones 39-45, tít. VI, constituciones 60-62.

Everywhere the rector ranked in importance and power next to the cloister over which he presided. His term was for a year only and two years must elapse before he could secure another term. The councillors, the above-mentioned special committee of the cloister, assembled with the outgoing rector in the chapter of the university every November 4, said a mass, and elected some doctor of more than thirty years of age from the community as rector. The viceroy took a hand only in the case of friction and wrangling.[3] Two years must elapse before this executive could be elected to succeed himself. At first, the post was open to both ecclesiastics and laymen (married and unmarried).[4] Later, married men were excluded and the ecclesiastics given an incidental but virtual monopoly of the rectorship,[5] although some provision was generally made for alternating between the laity and the cloth.[6]

The rector served without salary, but he enjoyed special perquisites. His jurisdiction was broad. He was commissioned to enforce order in the cloisters. In the realm of criminal jurisdiction the rector's powers accorded with the views of Alfonso the Learned[7] and reflected directly the *fuero* of

[3] *Recopilación de Leyes de los Reinos de las Indias*, lib. I, tít. xxii, leyes 4-6; *Constituciones de la . . . Universidad de México*, tít. II, constituciones 1-16. *Colección de reales cédulas sobre la Universidad de México*, No. 42. Madrid, 8 de febrero de 1646.

[4] *Ibid.*, No. 22, Campillo, 24 May, 1597.

[5] *Ibid.*, No. 47, Madrid, 31 July, 1656.

[6] J. de la Riva-Agüero, *La historia en el Perú* (Lima, 1910), p. 292.

[7] BNL, *Documentos del Virreinato*, XII, Cédula de su magestad en que contiene la jurisdicción del Rector de esta universidad,

Salamanca. Specifically, the rector had jurisdiction over the doctors, masters, officials, and students regarding not only their academic conduct but their criminal acts (while they were connected with the university), with the royal *audiencia* as an appellate court. Infractions punishable by mutilation or other serious corporal penalties fell, however, within the sphere of the state courts, to which the presiding officer of the university was obliged to supply evidence. And when it was discovered that the rectors of the universities of Mexico and Peru,[8] in conformity with medieval practice, could equip their two Negro lackeys with sidearms to be worn in the streets, great was the chagrin of the viceroys, archbishops, and regents of the *audiencias*, who were themselves denied so Janizarian a privilege.[9] The rector was sometimes persuaded by the archbishop to forego the actual practice in order to keep the sometimes touchy viceroy unruffled. Once in office the rector had, first of all, to conduct an official investigation of the financial management of the preceding administration or pay a smarting fine. He was to hold one of the three keys to the treasury,

Aranjuez, 19 de abril de 1589; *ibid.*, Alonso de Solórzano y Velasco, *Panegírico sobre los subjetos, pruebas y talentos de los Doctores y Maestros de la Real y Insigne Universidad de San Marcos* . . . (MSS., 1651), pp. 13-18.

[8] Real cédula, San Lorenzo, 24 de abril de 1618; *Constituciones* . . . (San Marcos de Lima), tít. I, constituciones 1-13; tít. II, constituciones 1-33.

[9] Solórzano, *op. cit.*, pp. 39-42. The doctors of San Marcos de Lima once petitioned for the preëminence which servants armed with swords would give them, saying the privilege would lead more men to seek the doctorate.

and to guard against the ever-present cheating and fraud. As a part of his duties he certified completed courses, took part in the acts and examinations of bachelors, attended all fiestas, funerals, and ceremonies honoring the doctors of the cloister, visited the professors once every two months, and fulfilled other obligations under pain of clearly specified fines and penalties.

The American descendant of the Spanish *scholasticus,* called the *maestrescuela,* was the liaison officer of the university and the cathedral church. In the pomp connected with the acts and examinations of candidates for higher degrees, for the integrity of which he was responsible, this official outranked the rector. He even designated the days for these acts. As supervisor of the incorporation into the cloister of persons with degrees from other institutions he was something of a censor. Where the *maestrescuela* did not exist all these functions were performed by a chancellor who also assumed the criminal jurisdiction reserved elsewhere for the rector.[10]

Among the ever-present and less important officers, the secretary, the treasurer, the bedels, the master of ceremonies, and the chaplain deserve mention. As archivist and keeper of records, the secretary filled an office which the historian appreciates most of all. The treasurer kept a record of income and expenditures and, in a book apart, a minute account

[10] *Constituciones* . . . (México), tít. V, constituciones 46-51; *Constituciones* . . . (Lima), tít. II, constituciones 28, 48; Méndez y Mendoza, *op. cit.,* I, 146-147. Full titles are repeated only at the beginning of each of the three sections.

of fees and fines of which he was custodian. The bedels—a combination of mace-bearers, errand boys, university police, janitors, and property men—conducted themselves with an air of importance and, possibly with the bare ability to read and write, cried out their announcements in the tongue of Caesar. The master of ceremonies was chief marshal at a time when placing persons in parades or seating them on the stage according to their rank was a matter of life and death. By the end of the colonial period the university of Mexico elected enough chaplains to say mass every day,[11] although the professor of propietary theology was required to say mass each month up until that time.

II

One may now turn to the relations of administrators to students, the requirements for admission, and the nature of student life.

Very rarely in the history of the university has there been such a unique situation as that into which these establishments were fitted. Colonial education was distinguished by its aristocratic nature. The university was nevertheless supported—at least after 1580—with an eye to the conversion and control of

[11] *Constituciones* . . . (México), tít. XXVI, constituciones 334-372; tít. XVIII, constituciones 373-382; tít. XXIX, constituciones 385-388; *ibid.*, (Lima), tít. I, constitución 7; tít. II, constitución 2; tít. VIII, constituciones 1-5; tít. IX, constituciones 9-17. Méndez y Mendoza, *op. cit.*, I, 147; Paz, *op. cit.*, p. 160; AGN, *Autos de Capellanías*, 1637-1782, I, application of Don Diego de Torres, *Provisiones de Capellanías*, 1783-1814, *Libro de Claustros*, 1734-1750, *Edictos para Provisiones de Capellanías*, 1805-1839.

the native as indicated by the inclusion of Indian languages in virtually all the American universities.[12] All candidates from the first were expected to be free from blood taint, a disqualification from which the sons of Indian chiefs were exempted in 1697. There was little effective prejudice against the Negro and the mulatto before the eighteenth century. The Indians were not excluded from the opportunity to attend the university and to receive degrees.[13] In reality the situation of the Negro and all types of mixed bloods was vastly different.

The drift of the times was indicated when the Count of Monclova (1688-1705) sanctioned the exclusion of Negroes, mulattoes and quadroons. The Marquis of Villagarcía forbade one to contest the chair of Medical Method in 1737 on the ground of his "note of infamy." Thus many who had hitherto enjoyed the highest privileges of colonial life were excluded. The rule against blood taint had not been enforced and some of these persons of color found their way into the professions, especially medicine, which was not held in high repute much before the nineteenth century. And when these "tainted" persons began to encroach upon the bar they were suddenly considered a menace in intellectual circles. In 1750 the viceroy, the Count of Castellar, prohibited the admission of mestizos, *zambos*, mulattoes, and

[12] Reales cédulas de 19 de septiembre y 23 de octubre de 1580.

[13] By a *cédula* of 12 March, 1697, it was declared that Indian chiefs and their descendants should be declared free from all blood taint. Vicente G. Quesada, *La vida intelectual en la América española* (Buenos Aires, 1917), p. 224. There was a special seminary to train Indians for the University of Guatemala.

quadroons to the university. A royal *cédula* of 1752[14] confirmed the harsh exclusion of Monclova and Castellar and left these unfortunates "chained by infamy." Many evidently did not yet choose to remain so chained by the superficial infamy of birth. The viceroy of Peru complained about the middle of the eighteenth century that the number of lawyers "of bad customs and obscure birth" who had arrived at professional dignity through the preparatory schools and scholarships in the universities warranted action. It was necessary to present certificates of racial purity[15] in order to enter the colleges and be graduated from the universities after Viceroy Manuel Amat (1761-1776).[16]

It was decreed from the outset in the constitutions of Mexico and Lima that no person whose father or grandfather had been punished by the Inquisition should be allowed to register in or graduate from the university. Indians, as "free subjects of His Catholic Majesty," by express stipulation were never excluded in Mexico and Peru. The 1775 edition of the constitutions of the University of Mexico still excluded the Negro, mulatto, "*Chino Moreno*," or any descendent of slaves.[17] Opposition to race discrimination was bound to result in a region where fusion was like a chromatic scale. The requirement

[14] Real cédula, Buen Retiro, 27 de septiembre de 1752.

[15] *Legitimidad y limpieza de sangre* was the Spanish phrase.

[16] *Memorias de los Virreyes*, IV (Lima, 1859), 479-481; Manuel Mendiburu, *Diccionario histórico-biográfico del Perú* (8 vols., Lima, 1874-1890), V, 543.

[17] *Constituciones de la . . . Universidad de México* (Mexico, 1775), tít. XVI, constitución 246.

of a certificate of pure blood enabled secret enemies to denounce and to exclude one from the benefits of education. Not infrequently the slow-moving machinery of justice finished the work of viciousness which malice had begun.[18]

In the remote sections and smaller universities social prejudice and race discrimination were slow to develop. Illegitimate persons even of pure race were usually not admitted to the more formal institutions.[19] The constitutions of the University of Córdoba, for instance, either intentionally or inadvertently kept complete silence on the question of blood purity as a prerequisite for degrees. It must be remembered, however, that the minor universities nearly always followed the constitution of one of the major universities including discriminatory provisions. Thus, when in 1710 an illegitimate person, apparently of pure race, petitioned to be granted a degree from the University of Córdoba, he was denounced, and received the degree from the cloister because of his character and improvement only because there was no specific statute, an oversight which was immediately corrected in the fundamental law.[20] For admission to the Caroline Academy in Chuquisaca, the most liberal wing of the

[18] AGN, *Informaciones de Limpieza de Sangre* (1 December, 1762 to 1768). An illustrative case is that of the family of Manuel Ramírez de Arelanno y Cervallo.

[19] The attitude toward bastardy in cases of worthy candidates varied from place to place.

[20] Archivo de la Universidad de Córdoba, *Libro de Claustros*, No. 1, claustros 36, 201, 202, 222, cited in Garro, *op. cit.*, pp. 159-160.

colonial universities, the same stipulation was made.[21] Yet in Córdoba, notwithstanding that the academic community professed to be scandalized when an illegitimate candidate passed himself off as legitimate, and despite the rigid statute, the cloister did occasionally confer degrees *in defectu natalium.*

Finally in the year 1804 the *cédula* of 1752, which had excluded mestizos, *zambos,* mulattoes and quadroons from the universities of Peru, was rescinded.[22] It was the growth of liberalism in Spain and the insurrections in America which finally lifted the racial bans altogether. After 1812 persons of color who could comply with all other requirements were permitted to matriculate in and graduate from all the universities, to assume the habit of religious communities, and to take sacred orders.[23] Unfortunately, it was now too late to be very "useful to the republic" to introduce Negroes and persons of mixed blood to ecclesiastical careers on a large scale.

Matriculation, after presentation of a certificate of sufficiency in rhetoric, was required of the students annually. It consisted of paying a fee of ten cents (two reales), half for the secretary and half for the treasurer. But it also meant a stipulation of the course the student proposed to take.[24] A maximum

[21] Paz, *op. cit.*, p. 236.

[22] H. Valdizán, "Los mestizos en la Universidad," *Boletín Bibliográfico de la Universidad de Lima,* Año VI, trimestre 1, cited in Valdizán, *La Facultad de Medicina de Lima* (3 vols., Lima, 1927-1929), III, 9.

[23] BNL, *Documentos del Virreinato del Perú,* No. 33, Order of the Cortes, Cádiz, 29 January, 1812.

[24] *Constituciones de la . . . Universidad de México,* tít. XVI, constitución 233; *Constituciones y Ordenanças de la Universidad*

period of forty days was allowed for this purpose.

The classes held in the morning, or *primas*, beginning at the awe-inspiring hour of seven o'clock, were regarded as most dignified. Those held in the afternoon, beginning at two-thirty o'clock, were known somewhat depreciatingly as vespers, or *vísperas*. The classes met every day and the professors in certain courses were required by university statute to give a lecture on at least one day in the week and sometimes more.[25]

In the arts course, in which the majority of undergraduates enrolled, the logic, metaphysics, and physics of Aristotle dominated until the late eighteenth century. In theology St. Thomas Aquinas and Duns Scotus reigned supreme. On Saturdays and Wednesdays a student championed a thesis.[26] These "acts," when they became formal, were known as conclusions in which one or more students defended a given thesis as a step toward the baccalaureate, licenciate, or doctorate. Picking points *(pique de puntos)*, an expression appearing so many times in the university records, consisted in selecting by chance certain questions to be discussed, usually twenty-four hours after the selection.[27] Sometimes these items were selected by the mere flick of the end of a pointer in the text, of which some very

y Studio General de la Ciudad de los Reyes del Piru (antiguas, Lima, 1602), tít. I, constitución 9; *ibid.* (modernas), tít. II, constitución 1.

[25] Méndez y Mendoza, *op. cit.*, I, 142-144.

[26] *Miercolinas* and *sabatinas*.

[27] *Lección de 24 horas.*

ornamental ones can still be found, or more frequently a child around seven or eight years of age inserted a knife between the pages of the volume of Aristotle or St. Thomas Aquinas from which the controversial matter was to be taken. Somewhat the same procedure was followed in final examinations and graduating exercises.

Due to the exceeding formality of Spanish colonial university life an oppressive routine prevailed. Incidental records reveal, however, what was inevitable; namely, that students act and march with decorum only a certain time and a certain distance. They were obliged by the constitutions to obey the rector, to attend all fiestas, parades and public acts, some of which called for caparisoned mounts and involved them in considerable expense. Scholars were permitted to select their own residences; however, they were subject to the rector in this matter and special statutory precautions were taken to prevent their falling into immoral surroundings. These houses were required to be above suspicion and free from all stigma. The rector not only kept a roll of the students in the houses, but that dignitary could, upon suspicion, order students to vacate any house and punish disobedience by expulsion from the university. Wearing apparel was not too personal a subject for regulation. Modest raiment, from which students frequently have a penchant to depart, was enjoined by the authority of the law, whose infractors were menaced with the dire penalty of suspension. Bright-colored stockings, gold passementerie, embroidery, side burns, and pompadours—which must have been off-color vanities of that day—were misdemeanors conspicuous enough to be expressly prohibited by the statutes of the university. Dressed in the long cloak and cassock, except in the case of physicians, one was required to complete the ensemble with the bonnet upon pain of suspension and loss of credit for courses.[28]

The admonitions of the Jesuits were most paternal and explicit. Among them, to prevent any artifices in display, the lining of cassocks had to be of the same color as the cassocks themselves. Nor could the poor aspirant of Academe wear short, loose sleeves (or *hungarina*) with trimmings or buttons or luridly colored doublets or jackets. Finally, in the strain of Polonius' injunctions to Laertes, the constitutions advise and require emphasis on the quality and manner of the use of clothes, which should "be modest in accordance with one's state, and not in accordance with one's levity and ease."[29] Of course formal academic dress and colors for the various degrees were required.

Carrying arms and indulging in nocturnal scandals were the bane of the university authorities from the time of Alfonso the Learned. It was therefore faithfully inserted in the laws that no student could attend classes equipped with either offensive or defensive arms. The student discovered in a violation was deprived of the weapons and denounced by the

[28] *Constituciones de la . . . Universidad de México,* tít. XVI, constituciones 225, 226.

[29] *Constituciones de la Universidad de Córdoba,* constitución 63.

rector. The arms were sold, one third going to the bedel, or whoever discovered and took them, and the other two thirds to the treasurer of the university. The offending scholar was then clapped in jail (as much a part of the university as the chemistry laboratory today) for eight days. Whoever resisted or refused to surrender his arms lost all credits for an entire year. Bail, loans, and illegal profits were circumscribed by royal laws. All members of the community were obliged to report any scandal to the rector for punishment. It was the custom to make stealthy and clandestine visits by night to apprehend students in any departures from the path of rectitude. Masters were expected to teach "the law of God," but they were not to rely too heavily upon its observance.

These were matters of caprice, but, in a society where so much emphasis was put upon family and marriage within the class, it is not surprising to find a royal prohibition of student marriages without parental consent.[30] As a guarantee to the state, and to the family, all requests for permission of students to marry—as in the case of army officers—had to be transmitted to the royal government through the rector. Marriages contracted without compliance with this law were declared null and void.

But the colonial university offered something of opportunity as well as restriction. Notwithstanding the fact that education was determined by the con-

[30] *Colección de reales cédulas sobre la Universidad de México*, Real cédula de 11 de junio de 1792; Méndez y Mendoza, *op. cit.*, I, 165.

ventional political and social tenets of religion and aristocracy, there was a strange and surprising respect for ability born in poverty. The University of San Marcos de Lima never limited the number of indigent white students who could receive the support or exemption from the fees of the institution. For every ten bachelors, a fellowship was awarded as a compensation for the successful cultivation of "the sciences" (all branches of learning), although it was not the custom to exclude the well-to-do from those to whom the rule might apply.[31] Mexico early developed the same custom of extending aid to the brilliant aspirant of impecunious family. The records of the institution are sprinkled with petitions for grants in aid, which, judged from their constant repetition, must have met with success.[32]

The Jesuit universities were more specific in the matter. At Córdoba, for instance, any student, having passed the requisite courses and acts in arts or theology, could be exempted from graduation fees by a vote of the full cloister, but for every degree gratuitously bestowed one had to be conferred upon another person amply qualified to make the stipulated outlay.[33] So many students sought

[31] John Tate Lanning, "Las universidades coloniales de Hispano-América en el desarrollo cultural y político del Nuevo Mundo," *Revista de la Universidad de Córdoba*, Año XVIII (1931), p. 17.

[32] Illustrative is the petition of Francisco Molinas for an *ayuda de costa*. *AGN*, *Autos Hechos sobre Diversas Materias, desde 1560 hasta 1700*, "pidimientos" Nos. 1 and 2. See also petition of José María Heredia, *ibid.*, *Certificaciones de Variedad de Asuntos, desde 1797 hasta 1827*.

[33] *Constituciones de la Universidad de Córdoba*, constitución 65.

exemption from such fees that after 1713 it was resolved that only three masters selected by chance for each course should graduate without expense *(pro universitate)*. Thereafter the students who drew their straws with bated breath proved harassingly numerous. Some of the frustrated ones interminably petitioned the whole cloister, some paid only half the fees, and others divided them with a second student who paid half.[34] All candidates for the master's degree in Córdoba, however, who could show convincing poverty, were, after unabating demands upon the university authorities, exempted from payment of fees. Six scholarships were maintained in the University of Chuquisaca and the two colleges there boasted a regular retinue of fellows.

Aid to the worthy student was in keeping with the policy of the crown in Charles III's time. In 1770 the universities of Spain and the Indies were ordered to grant certain degrees to those of the requisite merit who could not muster the fees.[35] Wherever the king's money was employed, however, the descendants of conquerors and sons of royal servants who had fallen upon evil days were preferred. And even college students petitioning the universities for examinations looking to degrees then joined the hue and cry.[36]

[34] Archivo de la Universidad de Córdoba, *Libro de Claustros*, No. 1, claustros 37, 41, 45, 59, 67, 82.

[35] *Ibid.*, Real cédula de 24 de enero de 1770; *Libro de Claustros*, No. 2, claustros 200, 233, 247, 257; *Libro de Claustros*, No. 3, claustros 289, 294, cited in Garro, *op. cit.*, pp. 157-159.

[36] Paz, *op. cit.*, pp. 169-170.

Nor did the approach of the struggle for independence hamper the system of student aid. San Carlos de Lima, one of the most progressive institutions training candidates for degrees, maintained seventeen scholarships in 1796, twelve supported by the crown and the rest by private individuals. At the opening of the nineteenth century scholarships in medicine and surgery were established in Lima upon the plea of Hipólito Unánue.[37] The nervousness of the crown over America in 1816 led, perhaps, to the creation of six fellowships for Latin Americans in Spanish institutions in Europe.[38] At the time this news reached America, as a further sign of emphasis on relief of the poor, students in the University of Caracas were being permitted to come to classes in whatever clothes their fathers could afford, to speak Castilian, and to assume a more emancipated attitude in scholastic debates.[39] Support to the indigent remained the steadfast policy of Spanish-American universities until the wars of independence completely deranged the financial provisions made for them. Far from being an innovation of a particular establishment, the system of fellowship was universal. From the humble college to the greatest major university it was an equally respected practice.

The conferring of the doctorate was impressive even in an age of unremitting pomp. On the after-

[37] H. Unánue, *Guía de 1796*, p. 206, in Jorge G. Leguía, *El Precursor* (Lima, 1922), p. 48.

[38] Real cédula de 25 de mayo de 1816, *Colección de reales cédulas sobre la Universidad de México*, No. 209.

[39] Méndez y Mendoza, *op. cit.*, I, 194-195.

noon before the investiture an impressive parade was held. In the front marched musicians with the perennial kettledrums and oboes, followed by the bedels with the maces of the university, the doctors in caps and gowns, the masters and the secretary, and finally the candidate between the senior member of faculty and the godfather. For the exercises of the following day, a stage was raised in the cathedral or church large enough to hold the cloister. There, in the midst of the royal, metropolitan, and family arms, was placed a table bearing the doctoral insignias, a book of the gospels, and urns for the fees. The godfather, chosen not so much for his Latin as his ability to pay the expenses when the actual father was poor, approached the rector and proposed in such Latin as he could memorize the thesis of his protégé. The candidate then stood up and disputed until the rector called a halt. After other ceremonial acts the godfather came forward once more, and, escorted by the bedels, conducted his charge before "his lordship" (rector) and, with another "brief and elegant" Latin oration, requested the degree. After a response from a doctor of the cloister, the candidate, if successful, knelt like the knights of old and, with his hands on the mass book, was dubbed doctor. The insignias, as partial compensation for his expense and trouble, were then attached to the new doctor by the godfather. Placing a ring upon the candidate's finger, and giving him a book as a symbol of the scholastic degree—each with the proper Latin injunction—the godfather took the candidate to his place in the salon, embraced him, and then gave way to such doctors and masters as were present, who embraced him in turn.[40] In the major universities the insignia were kept for a whole day on a plush cushion on the balcony of the godfather's house and the candidate rode in state with his protector to the investiture. All this was very expensive. Even in the Jesuit universities, bolstered up with their *Ratio*, a catalogue of detail and experience, abuses developed. They finally managed to limit the expense to 250 pesos. And in 1781, after the departure of the Jesuits, these costs were abolished altogether in Córdoba and Chuquisaca.[41] But in the University of San Marcos de Lima, during the decadent period in the eighteenth century, each rising doctor, after paying flat fees to the rector and other officers of the university, was also required to fee all the members of the learned community taking the trouble to attend the ceremony to which it was compulsory to invite them. If the degree were secular, each member of the cloister was given a velvet bonnet, and if ecclesiastical, one of cloth. In addition, the graduate gave each "six fat hens, four pounds of cold viands, and a pair of gloves." This outlay in San Marcos "united with the expences attendant upon the public exhibition of a bull fight, in the great

[40] *El Mercurio Peruano*, III, 241-243; Joseph Skinner, *The Present State of Peru* (London, 1805), pp. 170-171.

[41] *Constituciones de la Universidad . . . de los Charcas*, constitución 20, Paz, *op. cit.*, p. 159; *ibid.*, *de Córdoba*, constituciones 17, 20, 22, 31, 32, 33, 35, 38, 39, 40; Archivo de la Universidad de Córdoba, *Libro de Claustros*, No. 2, claustros 124, 130, 160, 245; Garro, *op. cit.*, pp. 136-137.

square, on the day of admission, and the sumptuous entertainment given to all present, were found, on an average estimate made in 1743 [the century of greatest decadence], to amount to the extravagant sum of ten thousand piastres for each degree."[42] Although efforts at reform finally lowered the figure to approximately 1,500 pesos, in the University of San Felipe in Santiago de Chile pretense was thrown down and degrees sold like a pair of shoes before and after instruction began.[43] With these evils, however, the reforms initiated under Charles III came to successful grips in the reign of his successor.[44]

Aside from the blanket oath *in licitis et honestis* upon matriculation to obey the king, the viceroy, and the rector, and to keep the faith pure, special oaths marked every significant step of the student's progress. As early as 1624 the very characteristic oath to defend the immaculate conception was required of graduates. Disrespect for the kingship attributed to the Jesuits prompted the Council of Constance to add the oath to abjure the "execrable doctrine" of tyrannicide and regicide. Students who had a vote in naming the professors to their chairs

[42] Skinner, *op. cit.*, p. 169. The grocery list in the University of San Felipe, given to the professors and doctors, included such delicacies as sweetmeats.

[43] ANC, Archivo de la Universidad de San Felipe, *Libro de Acuerdos*, No. 1, ff. 20, 25, 28, 56, 60, 61, 72, 86, 136, 145, 148, 159, 175, 188.

[44] BNL, *Documentos del Virreinato*, XXX, Real cédula, Aranjuez, 25 de marzo de 1801.

were subjected to an oath that they had made no commitments.[45]

Despite all handicaps, it appears that a surprising total of approximately 150,000 students received degrees from Spain's colonial universities. Due to the disappearance of the archives of the universities of Chuquisaca and Lima, and the clandestine conferring of degrees by the Jesuits, the exact number of graduates remains a matter of conjecture. Yet there are scraps of evidence, which, when thoroughly weighed, constitute a basis for an estimate which should be no perversion of the truth. The University of Mexico, holding an exclusive right to degrees in the viceroyalty,[46] conferred 29,882 bachelors' degrees and 1,162 higher degrees by 1775.[47] And from then until independence 7,850 bachelors' and 473 doctors' and licentiates' degrees were conferred.[48] The total figure was 39,367 degrees. Even then the number of higher degrees was regarded as lamentably low. And this figure does not include the candidates from Puebla, Oaxaca, Valladolid, Durango and Guadalajara who never came up to

[45] *Constituciones de la . . . Universidad de México*, tít. XVII, constitución 239; tít. XXXV, constitución 402; *Constituciones de la . . . Universidad de Lima*, tít. XIV, *constituciones* 3-5.

[46] Mérida de Yucatán excepted.

[47] *Constituciones . . .*, [1775] prólogo.

[48] AGN, *Actos de Repetición y Grados de Licenciados en Todas Facultades, desde 1775 hasta 1842; ibid., Grados de Bachilleres en Artes, desde 1794 hasta 1842; ibid., 1779-1794; Grados de Bachilleres en Facultad Mayor, desde 1770 hasta 1810; Grados de Bachilleres en Facultad Mayor, desde 1811 hasta 1842.*

the capital to go through the examinations and ceremonies of investiture. Facts and figures of this kind[49] do not make a tentative estimate of 150,000 unreasonable.

As already noted, academic chairs were created initially by the viceroy and *audiencia*,[50] but once under way the regular machinery was incorporated in the constitutions. Viceroys in later years sometimes created chairs, but after 1768 only with the express permission of the king,[51] which was always necessary to add a new professorship in the universities of the religious. The number of chairs which a university might have, ranged, in the case of Lima, from nine to forty.[52] In Lima, as in all the model universities, chairs were proprietary,[53] temporary, and substitute.

The chairs were won by competition. The temporary chairs were bestowed upon the winners of the compulsory[54] contest called "*oposición*," held every

[49] Some of the bases of this decidedly impressive figure are: Riva-Agüero, *op. cit.*, p. 294; Skinner, *op. cit.*, p. 171; AUC, *Libros de Grados*, *passim*; Méndez y Mendoza, *op. cit.*, I, 396; A. Fuenzalida, *La evolución sociale de Chile* (Santiago, 1906), pp. 264, 272-274; Archivo de la Universidad de San Felipe, *Libro de Indice*, *Libro de Grados*; René-Moreno, *op. cit.*, II, 26, 40; Valentín Abecia, "Adiciones a la matrícula de Velasco Flor," *Boletín de la Sociedad Geográfica de Sucre*, 1908, cuadros 1-4; Paz, *op. cit.*, pp. 398-399; Archivo de la Universidad de Córdoba, *Libros de Actas de Exámenes y Matrículas* (9 libros), 1670-1882.

[50] AGN, *Libro de Cátedras y Claustros, desde 1553 hasta 1561.*

[51] Unless provided for in the original charter.

[52] Luis A. Eguiguren, *Catálogo histórico del claustro de la Universidad de San Marcos, 1576-1800* (Lima, 1912), pp. 7-45.

[53] *De propiedad.*

[54] *Constituciones de la . . . Universidad de México*, tít. IV, constituciones 45, 47; *ibid.*, tít. XIII, constituciones 162-190.

four years except when the chairs were vacated by death, malfeasance, or resignation. In such cases after a meeting of the cloister, edicts of vacancy were posted in the university city. Edicts of vacancies in the proprietary professorships, usually occurring only upon the death of the incumbent, were posted outside the viceregal capital also. Candidates appeared before the rector to prepare for the ordeal of *oposición* some time later. The textbook used in the chair was produced and a child opened it with a knife. Within the limitations there presented the candidate might take his choice and register his points with the bedel for the benefit of disputants and hecklers. In the meantime aspirants could not talk to others, and if they chose to pay the cost, could set a guard upon their opponents. Enemies sometimes sent voting students to their houses under the guise of friendship to provoke them into conversation! If the chair involved was temporary, all candidates were heard on the same day; if proprietary, a separate day for each was set apart. The voters,[55] which included all accredited students and bachelors in the faculty, as well as doctors, licenciates, and masters not in the faculty, cast their ballots into an urn. The result was proclaimed by the authorities[56] and displayed upon he walls of the

[55] A candidate could demand the roster of voters. AGN, *Provisiones de la Cátedra de Theologia, 1570-1672; Autos hechos sobre la Prima de Theologia,* f. 193; *Provisiones de Cátedras de Canones, 1615-1678,* f. 43. In these cases the legitimate voters are listed.

[56] AGN, *Provisiones de Cátedras de Artes, 1569-1662; Constituciones de la . . . Universidad de México,* tít. XII, constituciones 158, 159-167, 170, 171-178, 186-190, 191-222.

university, the Tribunal of the Inquisition, and other public buildings.

This system was defective. Professors were so prone to succumb to the temptation to popularize and cater to the student's plebeian tastes that the system was in the long run changed in favor of a special commission of dignitaries of university, church, and viceroyalty, who filled all chairs except those of the Aquinas and Scotus (theology), which were filled by viceroy and confirmed by the king.[57]

But what was the compensation of the professoriate in the colonial universities? In the sixteenth century professors' salaries, which continued after retirement, ranged from one to two hundred pesos a year, although approximately the sum of 150 or 200 pesos continued to be the most usual consideration[58] to the eighteenth century when the ceremonies of the doctoral investiture sometimes cost the candidate ten thousand! And these salaries did not always come annually, but for many years were in the form of irregular and fractional stipends,[59] although the gratuities were frequent. The salaries in some chairs were as low in 1775 as in 1553, but the first chair of sacred theology, the most highly paid, enjoyed seven hundred pesos in Mexico in 1775. Notwithstanding that the tendency of the price scale was upward, academic incomes were virtually static, for

[57] By 1681. *Constituciones de la . . . Universidad de México*, note 22, p. 119.

[58] AGN, *Libro de Cátedras y Claustros, 1553-1561*, ff. 39-44.

[59] AGN, *Pagas de Catedraticos y Ministros*, 1657-1662, Rateo de Catedraticos, 1654.

many professors could claim only one hundred pesos *per annum* in 1800.[60] These figures frequently impinged, in spite of their immutable condition, upon such matters as the value of money in the vicinity. The salaries in San Marcos de Lima,[61] where one professorship netted 1,350 pesos *per annum*,[62] were approximately double those in Caracas. After taking into consideration the cost of living then and now, one must also remember that it has always been a tradition in Spanish countries that professors descended from the pulpit, the bench, or some governmental office—all remunerative posts—to hand on to students the specialized erudition of that particular walk of life.

Retirement pay for professors, as well as scholarships for worthy students, were provided in the colonial institution. In a typical case throughout the colonial period it was provided that he who had held a proprietary chair for twenty consecutive years and participated in a stipulated number of public acts, should retire with full pay minus sixty-five pesos[63] which, along with thirty-five from the university, went to pay the substitute professor who took his place in active teaching. A retiring professor lost no privileges, exemptions or honors, but he did not receive fees or participate in the acts of the univer-

[60] *Constituciones de la . . . Universidad de México*, tít. X, leyes 101-120.

[61] Eguiguren, *op. cit.*, *passim.*

[62] Méndez y Mendoza, *op. cit.*, I, 84-85.

[63] In Lima this deduction was one third of the salary of the proprietary professor. *Constituciones . . .* (Lima), tít. VI, constitución 61.

sity.[64] Retirement was not compulsory, although the professor usually reminded the authorities of the approaching date, and the professor could resume his old chair at will. Retirement provisions were made by the viceroy in conjunction with the cloister.[65] Toward the end of the eighteenth century service in both temporary and proprietary chairs was computed, while the rigors of the Mexican climate led to the inclusion of substitute time.[66] Although some universities followed the practice of Mexico[67] and Lima, others illustrate how varied was the practice. Professors in the University of Caracas, for example, were retired at the end of terms which ranged from twenty to forty-four years.[68] The wars of independence naturally threw the whole system seriously out of balance.

[64] *Constituciones de la . . . Universidad de México* (antiguas), f. 23, constitución 133; *ibid.* (modernas), tít. XI, constituciones 133-134.

[65] AGN, *Jubilaciones de Catedraticos*, 1613-1782, *passim.* See document, dated 3 July, 1678, and signed Plaza y Jaén.

[66] Real cédula, San Lorenzo, 8 de noviembre de 1738, *Colección de reales cédulas sobre la Universidad de México*, No. 123; Aranjuez, 17 de abril de 1742, *ibid.*, No. 129.

[67] AGI, 129-3-6, *Constituciones de la Universidad de San Felipe*, constitución 48.

[68] Méndez y Mendoza, *op. cit.*, pp. 394-396.

PHILOSOPHY

Chapter III

THE LAST STAND OF THE SCHOOLMEN

If the detractors of the Spain of the conquest have at last been measured by the rod of reason, those of Spanish colonial intellectual life still march with their measure untaken. And their number is both persistent and legion. Taken all together, they fall in line with the judgment of the relatively friendly Joseph Skinner who could not exempt the American institution when, in 1805, he said that "Abstract ideas, despicable chimeras, and vain subtleties, explained in a coarse and barbarous style, formed the proud and useless science which resounded" in the halls of the European universities.[1] After revolution had already shaken the Spanish Empire from Mexico to Buenos Aires, the Scotchman, Robert Semple, thought the American mind had advanced approximately to the standards reached in Spain exactly two hundred years before.[2] A similar lament marked the entire course of the nineteenth century, for in 1841 Rafael María Baralt calmly averred that "the names of Locke, Bacon, Galileo, Descartes, Newton, and Leibnitz, were never heard in the

[1] Joseph Skinner, ed. and trans., *The Present State of Peru* (London, 1805), p. 174.

[2] "Venezuela histórica en vísperas de la guerra de independencia —1810-1811—descrita por un escocés . . .," *Boletín de la Academia Venezolana de la Historia*, XV (1932), No. 60, cited by C. Parra León, *La filosofía universitaria venezolana* (Caracas, 1934), p. 154.

schools of America until the nineteenth century was far advanced."[3]

And Cornielle De Paux, in his philosophical researches on the Americans,[4] asserted with typical prejudice that when M. Louis Godin left the La Condamine equatorial expedition shortly before 1750 to teach in the University of San Marcos de Lima, there were no students who could understand him. As a Frenchman it would not have occurred to him that his Latin or Spanish might have been responsible. As the nineteenth century faded Father Agustín Rivera thought it sufficient proof of the entire absence of critical philosophy to quote two unrepresentative theses of a Mexican provincial college in a book which he had the temerity to call *La filosofía en la Nueva España*.[5]

And this current of opinion wove its unsubstantiated way even into the twentieth century. On the eve of the World War Felipe Barreda's history of the mind in viceregal Peru still smacked of the diatribe.[6] The influence of the legend has arrived at our very threshold in the facile assumptions and majestic denunciations of Blanco-Fombona,[7] and it

[3] Rafael María Baralt, *Resumen de la historia de Venezuela desde el descubrimiento de su territorio por los castellanos en el siglo XV hasta el año de 1797* (Paris, 1841), p. 384 *et seq.*, cited in Parra León, *op. cit.*, p. 156.

[4] *Recherches philosophiques sur les Américains.* 2 vols., Berlin, 1768-1769.

[5] Lagos, 1885.

[6] Felipe Barreda y Laos, *La vida intelectual de la colonia.* Lima, 1909.

[7] Rufino Blanco-Fombona, *El conquistador español en el siglo XVI.* Madrid, 1922.

has crossed our threshold in the school texts and the lay opinion of academic communities in the United States.

Unfortunately, the legend is founded upon considerable truth. Count Campomanes, governor of the Council of Castile in the epoch of Charles III's efforts to reform the University of Salamanca, may have made a damning and none the less acute observation on this point when he said: "One of the best reasons of the decay of universities is the antiquity of their foundation; because the plan of studies established at the commencement, not having afterward undergone any reform, it follows that they must retain the dross and impurities of the remote ages, and cannot be freed from them without the intellectual lights afforded by time, and by the discoveries of the eminent subjects of every part of the literary world."[8] The cloister of Salamanca may not have been unrepresentative when in 1771 it rejected modern philosophers and physicists because they "did not symbolize so much with revealed truths" as Aristotle and because their predecessors in the cloister had not sought to introduce a "more exquisite taste into sciences" and into the curriculum.[9] But by 1800 much had changed in Spain's American colonies.

What type of men could this static, decadent,

[8] Reply of Count Campomanes on the proposal to reform the studies of Salamanca: *Plan de Estudios dirigido a la Universidad de Salamanca por Antonio Villagordo, 1771.* Translation by Skinner, *op. cit.*, p. 173. *El Mercurio Peruano*, III, 248-250.

[9] *Ibid.*, pp. 248-249; Skinner, *op. cit.*, p. 176.

scholastic regime so beloved by these men of Salamanca produce? In ordinary circumstances the regimen produced men of stupendous rote memory, along with imposing but inappropriate and artificial allusions to the ancients and to the myths. These had long been the symbols of the "compleat" intellectual, the proudest result of education and the surest mark of the colonial scholar. Prodigies at thirteen or fourteen held degrees in law, practiced before the royal *audiencia,* and competed against their professors for their posts. Such were the proud incidents selected by the editor of the constitutions of the University of Mexico to embellish the new edition of 1775.[10] Now this prodigious rote memory goes hand in hand with the general philosophical principle of authority which, unless carefully and constantly trimmed, is likely to go hand in hand with superstition. This decadent discipline not only immobilized the mind; it paralyzed the arts. When the language, subject, interpretation, meter and number of words had been settled by cartel in a poetical *certamen* the rest was left to the genius of the poet.

It was against the contingency of the defeat of this system that the uncompromising scholastics made their last stand. But innovation crept so gradually and so stealthily upon them that it was too late when they came to gird their loins for battle. The Americans, who on their own authority[11] were

[10] *Constituciones de la Real y Pontificia Universidad de México* (Mexico, 1775), introducción.

[11] There is considerable direct evidence on this point. AGG,

eclectics, were an ideal public for the Spanish Father Benito Gerónimo Feijóo (1676-1764) who, as a temperate Cartesian familiar with Newton and assailant of authority, became a good philosopher of transition, for, without professing a system of his own, he could say, as it was said of Homer: "What he thought he might require he went and took." His *Teatro crítico* and his *Cartas eruditas* became so popular in Quito that the prices soared above the already forbidding levels. Although there is no basic documentary evidence such as can be found in Mexico, Venezuela, and Guatemala, all authorities state without equivocation that René Descartes (1596-1650), Gottfried Wilhelm von Leibnitz (1646-1716), and Sir Isaac Newton (1642-1727) were taught in Quito as early as 1736 while the La Condamine expedition was in the presidency.[12] Unless there was unusual interdependence among them, the case is too impressive to be ignored. To Francisco Xavier Santa Cruz y Espejo (d. 1796), the great intellectual and precursor of Ecuador, this easy-

A1, 3-12, 12810, 1927, thesis (bachelor of philosophy) of Valerio Flores, 22 December, 1791: Potamonica sive Eclectica secta omnibus preferenda. *Ibid.*, 12823, 1932, thesis of Francisco García, 22 February, 1802: Phylosophia hominum enixa auctoritate insaniae, adscribi debet. Eclectica ergo phylosophandi methodus omnibus praeferenda.

[12] See Isaac Barrera, *Quito colonial* (Quito, 1922), and Pedro Fermín Cevallos, "Ecuatorianos ilustres: Padre Juan Bautista Aguirre," *El Iris . . .*, Quito, 5 November, 1861. Federico González Suárez, *Historia general de la República del Ecuador* (9 vols., Quito, 1890-1903), VII, 57, 61; *Resumen de la historia del Ecuador* (6 vols., Lima, 1870), II, 343, 344, 350; Rafael Altamira, *Historia de España y de la civilización española* (4 vols., Barcelona, 1900-1911), IV, 816-817.

going Spanish philosopher, Feijóo, was the center of the world of thought. With others his position was still more extravagant. To General Ignacio Escandón the new paladin was "the honor of the glories of Spain and even of the world, the beloved Adonis of America, and his adored master."[13] Humboldt was no less surprised to find the *Teatro crítico* than Abbé Nollet's *Traité d'électricité*.[14] The great encyclopedist, Pedro Peralta Barnuevo (1663-1743), corresponded with Feijóo as well as with the French Academy of Sciences.[15]

When the first skirmishes of the experimentalists with the Schoolmen were over, a vehement attack on Aristotle invariably indicated that the real battle to dethrone scholasticism was joined. It mattered not that other masters might have been more appropriately attacked. Aristotle was a pagan. What was more he was a symbol, and the conception of stagnation symbolized had been thrust upon him. Around 1758 the Conde de Peñaflorida proceeded dangerously near buffoonery when he called "Señor Aristotle" the "Marquis of Accidents, the Captain-General of the Occult . . ., and perpetual Alcalde Mayor of a Preadamite World."[16] Another Spaniard, the distinguished disciple of Pierre Gassendi (1592-1655), P. Tomás Vicente Tosca (1651-1723), was

[13] . . . *Un corto panegyrico . . . al querido Adonis de la America, a su adorado Maestro: el ilustrissimo Señor, y Rmo. P. Mro. D. Benito Geronymo Feyjoo* . . . . Lima, 1765.

[14] A. Humboldt, *Voyage aux régions équinoxiales du nouveau continent* (3 vols., Paris, 1811-1829; 13 vols., Paris, 1816-1832), III (1817), 142-143, cited in Parra León, *op. cit.*, p. 75.

[15] Suárez, *op. cit.*, VII, 57.

[16] Parra León, *op. cit.*, p. 42.

celebrated because he dissipated "the fear of the name of Aristotle." To defeat Peripateticism through Aristotle now became an obsession. Wipe it away and unhampered philosophy could be written on a *tabula rasa.* In a celebrated dispute in Venezuela in 1770 it was an ecclesiastic, A. de Valverde, who used the opportunity of a controversy with the Conde de San Xavier, renowned professor and literatus, to flail the first son of Stagira. To Valverde, Aristotle was "wicked," and his philosophy a bottomless "sink of errors," prejudicial alike to theology and the sciences. Aristotle was no aid to an understanding of nature and his authority was, therefore, "an irrational and tyrannical yoke never equalled by monarch." Curiously deferential to the Angelic Doctor, Valverde declared that Thomas Aquinas "did not learn from the infamous books of Aristotle." Refusing to be swerved by lampoons, moderates like San Xavier followed Johann Gottlieb Heineccius (1681-1741). They would not be partisans of Aristotle's *Physics,* adjudged his *Metaphysics* to be obscure, and yet could see no reason why they could not be guided by the *Dialectics* and the *Art of Poetry.*[17] Aristotle, exclaimed the outraged *oidor* of the *audiencia* of Lima, Ambrosio Cerdán y Pontero, is like "a certain Lagivia fish which, when pursued, gives off a dark fluid. . . ."[18]

[17] For a letter on this affair from Valverde to Xavier, Caracas, 7 August, 1770, see *Archivo del General Miranda* (14 vols., Caracas, 1929-1933), VII, 272-289.

[18] November 10, 1791, *Mercurio Peruano,* VIII, 148. This is a part of the evidence being used by Mr. William Dale in the preparation of a treatise on the intellectual revolution in Peru.

As the fight became less impassioned, it turned from Aristotle in particular to Peripateticism in general. Baltasar Marrero, a completely modern spirit, followed Valverde. The new crusaders were more moderate, for they knew that their object was not merely a just wrath, but freedom to observe nature. Such a man was Eusebio Llano Zapata who, in 1758, attacked the out-moded scholastic rigmarole "as abstractions and thoroughly useless disputes." The classroom circumventions and sophistries of his day "were magician's tricks . . . to deceive boobies and to seduce the unwary." Why should youth, he asked, be subjected to such loss of time and ruin of genius when there was every indication that an intellectual system based more solidly upon nature would result in unprecedented cultural growth?[19] Like discontent reached the provincial universities of Huamanga and Cuzco where Dr. Ignacio Castro in 1771 declared that in physics "ideas should conform to nature and not nature to ideas," for, he veritably preached, "the vague notions of Peripateticism . . . have never explained a single phenomenon of nature."[20]

Such advocacy did not go unrequited, for in that decade Juan de Soto, a professor in the University of San Marcos de Lima, surveyed the systems of

[19] Eusebio Llano Zapata to the Marqués de Villa Orellano, Cádiz, 25 June, 1758. See Eusebio Llano Zapata, *Memorias histórico-apologéticas de la América meridional* (Lima, 1904), pp. 597-598.

[20] Cited by Barreda y Laos, *op. cit.*, p. 328. See also D. César A. Ugarte, "Las universidades menores del Perú," *La Revista Universitaria del Cuzco*, Año VI (1917), No. 19, pp. 11-12.

Descartes and Gassendi and accepted some of the conclusions of Newton whose system had already been presented to the cloister by Federico Bottoni before Newton's death.[21] From this public teaching it was but a step to official toleration. In the year of Castro's outburst the Convictory of St. Charles was being welded from the ruins of the Jesuits. Under the distinguished liberalism of Rodríguez Mendoza (1750-1825),[22] so largely responsible for putting the words of René Descartes and Etienne Bonnot Condillac (1715-1780) in the mouths of Peruvian youth, it finally set a pace for higher education in Lima probably not paralleled elsewhere in the Americas. The viceroy, Don Manuel de Amat y Junient, in eager imitation of Charles III, actually insisted that at least one author in modern philosophy should be taught. But, in order not to replace one dogmatic authority with another, he declared for intellectual freedom when he asked the cloister of San Marcos to permit the students to accept any system of philosophy, or combination of philosophies, which appealed to them.[23] Similar liberty of intellectual systems was decreed by the American-born Viceroy Juan José Vértiz (1777-1784) in Buenos Aires. Henceforth Peru was distinctly in the modern age.

In their theses the Peruvian students showed

[21] Barreda, *op. cit.*, p. 310.

[22] Jorge Guillermo Leguía, *El Precursor*. Lima, 1922. "De un acto público de filosofía y matematicas, dedicado a la real Universidad de San Marcos, y breve extracto de las teses que ofreció sustentar el Actuante," *Mercurio Peruano*, VIII, 184-205.

[23] *Ibid.*, p. 187.

themselves the cultural descendants of Sir Isaac Newton,[24] while a lecturer in philosophy, Father Isidoro Celis, first prepared mathematical tables of the new discoveries in 1781 and published a celebrated compendium of the mathematics and physics of the renowned Englishman in 1787.[25] Moreover, José Baquíjano, aroused by the groans of the men who followed Tupac Amaru, used the occasion of his inaugural panegyric on Viceroy Agustín Jáuregui in 1781 to draw in bright and arresting colors the conditions of the natives. And he added that benevolent despotism was not enough, for "To better man against his will has ever been the deceitful pretext of tyranny."[26] After 312 copies of this address were found and finally sent to Spain, the reluctant authorities at last promised to burn the other copies turned up. Even then they took note only of Baquíjano's criticism of the Spanish conqueror, but the evolution of thought has eased over inexorably from the nature of essence to the nature of political justice—a fact of widespread and singular import on the eve of a wave of revolutions.[27] If it

[24] "Actuaciones escolásticas," *Mercurio Peruano*, VIII, 182 *et seq.*

[25] *Elementa philosophiae quibus accedunt principia mathematica verae phisicae prorsus necesaria.* Madrid, 1787.

[26] José Baquíjano, *Elogio del excelentísimo Señor Don Agustín de Jáuregui* . . . . Lima, 1781. See J. T. Medina, *La imprenta en Lima* (4 vols., Lima, 1904-1907), III, 106-115; *Memorias de los Virreyes* (Teodoro de Croix), V, 85-86.

[27] Baquíjano, whether it was against his will or not, became the leader of the liberal forces, and the symbol of reform. Take, for example, a verse of his welcome to Cuba:

Ilustra su periódico indigente
Con sabias producciones;
Asóciate á su gente,

were necessary to multiply evidence of this kind,[28] it could be shown that in the University of Chuquisaca, invariably dubbed the cerebrum of the revolution, there existed a more congenial intellectual atmosphere than in Lima.[29] José Miguel Juridi y Alcocer in Mexico greeted the nineteenth century with a course, still inedited, in "modern philosophy."

But this is the general evidence of the decline of the Schoolmen. Of concrete evidence on minute points there is no lack. A new photographic collection of manuscript and printed theses from the university archives of Mexico, Guatemala, Caracas, Chile, and Córdoba, illustrating all possible philosophies held from 1750 to 1810 has, in the course of the last decade, grown beyond five thousand. And they have almost entirely escaped the attention of the late José Toribio Medina. Although these theses were nearly always discreet, they were published without viceregal license.[30] Once one penetrates the very stilted and somewhat Castilian Latin

---

E instrúyela en útiles nociones,
Y pues eres de sabio noble forma
Influye en sus estudios la reforma.

Pedro de Lojaisar, "Elogio Poético del Dr. D. José Baquíjano y Carillo," *Mercurio Peruano,* IX, 175, notes 1 and 2.

[28] Vicuña Mackenna, *La revolución de la independencia del Perú, desde 1809 a 1819* (Lima, 1860); pp. 69-81, 258-260. D. Casiromi, "El Dr. D. Hipólito Unánue: ensayo biográfico," in Manuel de Odriozola, *Colección de documentos literarios del Perú,* VI (11 vols., Lima, 1863-1877), 535-548.

[29] Gabriel René-Moreno, *Los últimos días coloniales en el Alto-Perú* (2 vols., Santiago de Chile, 1896-1901), I, 162-191.

[30] José Toribio Medina's works on the press could be considerably extended by this source.

in which they are shrouded, and manages to remember that the specific ideas and discoveries of the moderns can be found within the scholastic formulae, the intellectual fermentation can no longer be left in doubt. Between the old and the new there could be no compromise on the fundamental problem of authority. To authoritative pronouncements the gauntlet was laid down by the new ideology for deadly combat. Henceforth the authority of mortals should not go unexamined—*Auctoritas humana examinis immunis esse non debet.*[31] Some came out boldly and condemned opinions thought out in a former age as contrary to universal nature,[32] and in logic the "frequent cause" and "fecund mother" of errors. *Nimia in sapientum auctoritatem deferentia errorum est fecunda mater.* Or, *Sapientum auctoritatis non raro est causa.*[33] There was always, however, a sharp contrast between natural and divine

[31] AUC, expediente "J.M.J.—*Concurso de grados de Bachiller en Artes del Curso que principió a leer el Dr. D. Baltasar Marrero a 18 de septiembre de 1788 y terminó el Doctor Don Francisco Antonio Pimentel a 6 de marzo de 1791,*" thesis of Manuel González, quoted in Parra León, *op. cit.*, p. 73. AGG, A1., 3-12, 12810, 1927, thesis of Valerio Flores, 22 December, 1791: Ut de humana auctoritate merito duvitemur sufficit Auctorem fallere posse aut falli.

[32] AGN, *Grados de Doctores y Licenciados en Todas Facultades, desde 1810 hasta 1816*, thesis of Agustín Madrid, 3 February, 1814: Opinio de mundi Optimismo, superiori saeculo excogitata, Numino summo iniuriae est, naturaeque universae.

[33] AUC, *Grados en Artes*, thesis of Manuel de Arnal. *Ibid.*, thesis of Raimundo García de Roa. Parra León, *op. cit.*, p. 74. It is to be regretted that the theses collected by Parra León are generally dated only 1788-1821. All theses from Caracas have come to me through this work. A check is now being started by the author and the essential data will be included in future publications.

authority. Some onslaughts on the principle were weakened by careful but natural hedging. "*In the natural,*"[34] not authority but experiment, "reason and experience," should be followed. *In rebus naturalibus non auctoritatis sed experientiae rationumque momenta sequenda sunt.*[35]

So even the testimony and authority of the Holy Fathers was limited by the strict requirements of the physical universe.[36] In purely philosophical matters the authority of the Fathers was in strict ratio to their persuasiveness and advantages as witnesses and was not to be considered an irrefragible argument. *In rebus pure philosophicis authoritas Sanctorum, tum plures, tum pauci sint, non nobis esse firmo, ac irrefragabili argumento.*[37] It was in strict imitation of Descartes to admit theological dogma "in the higher sense" and to proceed calmly to an explanation of the world on a physical basis.

If truth transcended the authority of the Holy Fathers, then it follows as the night the day that the truth, notwithstanding jesting Pilate, should be exalted as an absolute value for itself. It was gen-

[34] Italics mine.

[35] AUC, *Grados en Artes,* thesis of José Manuel Vargas. AGG, A1. 3-12, 12820, 1930, thesis of Pascual López y Plata, 27 October, 1799: In rebus physicis observationes, ac experimenta sunt consulenda.

[36] AUC, *Grados en Artes,* thesis of Antonio Rojas Queipo: Sanctorum Patrum auctoritas in rebus physicis non est praeferenda Doctoribus, in hac praecipue materia probatis.

[37] *Ibid.,* José Ignacio de Rivera, April, 1801. AGG, A1., 12810, 1927, thesis of Michale Aragón, 23 August, 1791: Sanctorum Auctoritas, sive paucorum, sive plurium in conclusionibus pure phylosophycis certa argumenta non supperdita; sed tantum pollet, quantum eorum persuacerit ratio.

erally recognized and sporadically stated that there were factors in the physical world which proceeded like a great silver rope along an inexorable course through all phenomena regardless of the opinions, prophecies, and systems of mortal men. From Socrates' *Phaedo,* Anselm, Descartes, and Newton's *Principia Mathematica* to the *Communist Manifesto* and *Capital* of Karl Marx and *Introduction to the Principles of Morals and Legislation* of Jeremy Bentham, it has been the dream of philosophers not only to discover and master this majestic cable of nature, but to reduce individual and social behavior to equally scientific and definitive rules. Scholar, potentate, and priest could not but listen with an agreeable disposition and admire wisdom, whether it flow from the lips of saint or idiot.[38] Thus solidly was built the framework of a generation of pioneers.

Strong evidences of a distinction between the traditional and the new rationalism cropped out on every hand. Once the students had begun to depend upon the experimental method, they were constrained to reduce their *a priori* material to a minimum. And what was more natural than the system of methodical doubt of the French philosopher and mathematician, René Descartes, in which it was possible to doubt everything down to existence? But *Cogito ergo sum!* The system of methodical doubt came to be accepted, if not actually followed, everywhere in America between 1736 and 1800.[39]

[38] AUC, *Grados en Artes,* thesis of José María Aguado: Veritas est admiranda quamvis idiota recenseatur. Parra León, *op. cit.,* p. 74.

[39] AGN, *Libro de Gobierno, desde 1796 hasta 1800,* thesis of

But by what criteria could a skeptic recognize the truth? The answer came overwhelmingly: in the things of the senses the best criterion of truth is the senses. *Sensuum testimonium circa res sensibiles est optimum veritatis criterium.*[40] For many years, however, there were those still disposed to rely exclusively upon the old dialectic tools of logic or evidence, "purified through the rules of logic"[41] and reason.[42] Although the acceptance of the senses as the criterion of truth emerged from this academic gristmill considerably modified, the modification was not based exclusively upon lingering classical dialectics. How many a modern philosopher, Bishop

---

Raimundo Ruiz, 31 July, *circa* 1799: Regula Cartesiana circa methodum est admittenda. For the above quotation, see AGG, A1., 3-12, 12821, 1931, thesis of Cayetano Bedoya, 1800. *Ibid.*, 12827, 1933, thesis of Vicente Merino, 13 August, 1804: Cartesiana methodus est admittenda. AUC, *Grados en Artes*, thesis of José Vicente Jaén.

[40] AGG, A1., 3-12, 12813, 1928, thesis of José Emanuel Alcántara, 30 January, 1794. *Ibid.*, 12826, 1933, thesis of Christóbal de Royas, 4 May, 1804: Sensus intimus infalibile veritatis Criterium. *Ibid.*, thesis of Francisco Rivas, 14 August, 1804: Testimonium sensuum circa res sensibiles firma veritatis regula. AGN, *Libro de Grados de Doctores y Licenciados en Todas Facultades, desde 1817 hasta 1829*, document dated 10 April, 1821: In rebus sensibilibus evidentia sensuum est optimum veritatis criterium.

[41] AGN, *ibid.*, desde 1786 hasta 1794, thesis of José Amato Gutiérrez: Veritatis criterium, seu Lydius lapis, quo verum a falso secernitur extat in regulis Logicalibus. *Ibid.*, *Gobierno*, 1793-1795, XXV, thesis of Melchior Velarde, 27 April, 1793: Evidentia est criterium veritatis omnis philosophiae, tum Metaphysica, tum physica, tum Moralis, unaqueque in ordine suo. *Ibid.*, *Libro de Grados de Doctores y Licenciados en Todas Facultades, desde 1795 hasta 1799*, thesis of Abundo Taionera, 22 January, 1797: Criterium viritatis est ipsa evidentia per regulas Logicae adplicata.

[42] *Ibid.*, *Gobierno*, *1796-1800*, XXVI, thesis of Rafael Céspedes, 28 January, 1800: Pro veritatibus intelligilibus dijudicandiis opimum criterium est evidentia rationis.

George Berkeley (1685-1753) in particular, has befuddled the brain by doubting the evidence of the senses and the existence of matter?[43] And there were those in the Indies, including Andrés Bello of the nineteenth century, who agreed with much of the subtle Bishop's dialogues.

But these problems were trivia and by-products of the profound victory of methodical doubt. The seemingly puerile elements of Cartesian philosophy which we reject so smugly today were also scorned by the colonial scholar. The Cartesian difficulty was the union of extension and matter or motion and mind to make it possible for the mind, or soul, as they said, to act upon the bodily members so as to create activity. Since Descartes was a man who thought it wise to disbelieve everything, it was singularly naïve of him, with no evidence at all, to achieve the union of body and mind in the pineal gland. This ridiculous notion American scholars rejected with uninterrupted consistency. *Anima non stat in conario Glandulae pinealis in medio cerebri constituta. . . .* It is little wonder that many familiar with the new systems regarded the Peripatetic explanation of the association of the mind and body as plainly superior.[44] To some the Aristotelian con-

[43] AUC, *Concurso de Grados* (1788-1791): Experientia physica potest esse erronea. AGN, *Libro de Gobierno, desde 1784 hasta 1792*, XXIV, thesis of José Feliz Muñatonez, 26 October, 1790: Materia non habet propriam existentiam. *Ibid.*, thesis of Felipe Ramos y Cervantes, 23 February, 1791: Explosis quamplurimis Philosophorum placitis, corporis naturam in pluralitate partium collocamus. *Ibid.*, 1796-1800, XXVI, thesis of Mariano Rosario, 7 January, 1800: Scientia materiae ignota est.

[44] AGN, *Libro de Gobierno, desde 1793 hasta 1795*, XXV, thesis

ception which placed the mind in all parts of the body was sufficient; others averred the brain was the seat, and others did not profess to know exactly how the mind joined the body.[45]

The cerebrum governed the body through an organ made sensible.[46] The Cartesian position that when the mind feels the motion upon which sensation depends impressed upon the sensory nerves, it is passed to the cerebrum where sensation is perfected,[47] was everywhere defended. Occasionally "the animal spirits," or "subtle and elastic vapors" were debated as the means of conducting impressions.[48] Notwithstanding, the general conviction was

of Emanuel Barcena, *et al.*, 27 May, 1793: De comertio animae, et corporis Peripateticum systema caeteris ut longe probabilius.

[45] AGG, A1., 3-12, 12897, 1924, thesis of Michael Marín, February, 1785: Anima non stat in conario Glandulae pinealis in medio cerebri constituta; sed tota in toto corpore, et tota qualibet eius parte. *Ibid.*, 12797, 1924, thesis of José María Piñol, 9 December, 1785: Anima non in conario glandulae pinealis solummodo est ut opinati sunt Recentiores, sed etiam in toto corpore, et qualibet ejus parte est. AGN, *Libro de Gobierno, desde 1796 hasta 1800*, thesis 19 May, 1797 (?): Anima precipue residet in cerebro. *Ibid.*, thesis of Juan Altamirano, 17 August, 1799: Et Animam in corpus, et corpus in animam physice influere contendimus quo vero modo illud fiat ignoramus. *Ibid.*, *Grados de Doctores y Licenciados en Todas Facultades, desde 1810 hasta 1816*, thesis of Agustín Madrid, 3 February, 1814: Cerebrum nostrum animae sedem esse putandum est.

[46] AGN, *Grados de Doctores y Licenciados en Todas Facultades, desde 1808 hasta 1809*, thesis of Ignacio Michael Patiño, 11 January, 1808: Nulla erat sensatio sine organi mutatione a sensibili facta.

[47] AGG, A1., 3-12, 12815, 1929, thesis of Ignacio Perdomo, *circa* January, 1795: Qualibet animae sensatio pendet a motu nervorum, qui a medio cerebro orti in sensum organa terminantur.

[48] AUC, *Grados en Artes*, thesis of Feliciano Montenegro, quoted in Parra León, *op. cit.*, p. 79: Sensatio ibi facta (in retina) differtur

that the spiritual commerce of mind and body was achieved only in man[49] whom thought lifted above mere mechanisms.

To put the connection on a purely physical basis as Condillac and John Locke (1632-1704) did, left man in a class with animals, enjoying the same union of mental and physical. To extricate the philosophers from this implication that brutes were made in God's own image the mechanists appeared. Some Americans, following the mechanists' lead, declared that the lower animals were mere *automata*, that the brute *anima* was material and divisible[50] without the capacity to think and to feel. With as much ingenuity as timidity, others sought to escape by placing the soul of animals in an intermediate position be-

ad usque cerebrum per spiritus animales nervis vagantes. AGG, A1., 3-12, 12799, 1926: *Assertiones philophiae mentis, et sensuum mechanicae, ad usus physicos accommodatae: atque aliae physico-theologicae juxta mentem recentorum propugnandae* (Guatemala, 1788), p. 15: Beluarum anima diversa non est ad ea subtilissima, maximeque actuosa substantia, quae vitalium & animalium spirituum nomine vulgo designatur.

[49] AGN, *Libro de Gobierno, desde 1793 hasta 1795*, XXV, thesis of Bernardino Cantú, 13 April, 1793: Mens humana est substantia spiritualis . . . . AUC, *Grados en Artes*, José Isidoro Avila: Solus spiritus est sensationis capax.

[50] AGN, *Libro de Gobierno, desde 1793 hasta 1795*, XXV, thesis of José Magro, 18 April, 1793: Anima Brutorum animalium est estensa et dibisibilis. AGG, A1., 3-12, 12798, 1925, thesis of Rafael Barroeta, 27 April, 1787: Bruta pensatione gaudere omnimodo defensabo, et etiam cum contrariis esse pura machina defendo. *Ibid.*, 12822, 1931, thesis of José Antonio Rivera, 30 April, 1801: Cum Belluis non detur nec cogitatio ulla, nec sensatio, non est in eis anima spiritualis. *Ibid.*, 12824 1932, thesis of José Francisco Barrundia, 19 February, 1803: Nulla in Belluis anima spiritalis invenitur. Sensatione & cogitatione carent.

tween material and spirit.[51] But the bulk of the weight was against the soul of animals. Some even went so far as to hold that between animals and vegetables there was no essential distinction.[52] It is little wonder that others despairingly rejected all theories of the conjunction of soul and body.[53]

The difficulty into which Descartes had thrust the world in setting up intercourse between soul-thought and body-extension was thus handled *ad absurdum* by the colonial thinkers. Arnold Geulincx (1624-1669) had sought a *deus ex machina* to escape the dilemma entirely through his "occasional causes," for, upon any impact upon the senses, "God caused" a responsive action. When Descartes' innate ideas[54] were rejected, as they always were in the Indies, it was possible to consider God not only the occasional cause, but with Nicholas Malebranche (1638-1715) to "see all things in God."[55] Outside of Caracas,[56]

[51] AGN, *Grados de Doctores y Licenciados en Todas Facultades, desde 1810 hasta 1816*, thesis of Mariano Ferriz, 7 January, 1812: Anima Brutorum est substantia materiam inter, et spiritum intermedia.

[52] AUC, *Grados en Artes*, thesis of Santiago Limardo: Vegetalia inter et animalia nulla existit differentia essentialis, ac necessaria.

[53] *Ibid.*, thesis of Cristóbal Hurtado de Mendoza: Animae et corporis commercium nullum systema expedisse: omnia ergo rejicienda.

[54] AGG, A1., 3-12, 12830, 1934: *Theses ex universa philosophia quas D. Joannes Firminus de Ayzinena et Piñol ad bachalaureatum ascendens defendabat* . . . (Guatemala, 1786), p. 5: Neque existunt aliquae ideae nobiscum innatae, seu concreatae, ut dici solet. AGN, *Libro de Gobierno, desde 1793 hasta 1795*, thesis of 19 November, 1793: Nullae dantur ideae mentibus nostris innatae in sensu Cartesianorum.

[55] AGG, A1., 12792, 1921, thesis of Emanuel González, 1766: Deus phycice praemovet causas nesesarias ad operamdum.

[56] AUC, *Grados en Artes*, thesis of Pedro Ignacio de Echuzuría, quoted in Parra León, *op. cit.*, p. 85: Ad explicandum mentis cum

however, students made short shrift of occasionalism which was "incompatible with free will and liberty and unworthy of a philosopher."[57]

As a modern philosopher, John Locke hardly appeared more important than merely one of the disciples of Descartes. Luis Antonio Verney (1713-1792), the Portuguese intermediary and eclectic so popular in the Indies, accepted Locke on the "origin of ideas."[58] The fact that Locke endowed matter with the faculties of mind, so universally associated with the spirit, and was at the same time accepted in many places, indicates that perhaps he was not everywhere fully understood. Accepting the "fibres" and "nervous fluid" as the transmitting elements between the senses and the cerebrum, Locke made them and not the pineal gland the seat of the celebrated union of which too much has already been said. Since all the material ideas had to come over these channels from the senses, it was clear that "whatever is, was

corpore commercium causarum occasionalium systema praeferendum est.

[57] AGG, A1., 3-12, 12813, 1928: *Philosophicae propositiones defendae, pro baccalaureatus gradu in eademmet facultate obtinendo A. D. Joanne Michaele de Fiallos . . .*, Guatemalae, die XI. mensis Februarii anno Dni. M.DCC.XCIV, p. 8: Cartesii ac Malebranchii *causarum occasionalium* hypotesis nec Philosopho digna est, nec rectae Theologiae consentit. AGN, *Libro de Gobierno, desde 1784 hasta 1792*, thesis of Felipe Ramos, 23 February, 1791: Res naturales haud sunt causae occasionales, ut Cartesiani edocent, sed habent foecunditatem, Aenergiam, vim agendi sive veram effectricem virtutem.

[58] Luis Antonio Verney, *Verdadero método de estudiar para ser útil a la República y a la Iglesia . . .* (Portuguese edition, 1746; Spanish translation of José Maymo y Ribes, Madrid, 1760), II, letter 8, III, letter 10.

first in the senses."[59] But Locke was apparently more popular in Venezuela.[60] Likewise he was among the first to bear the brunt of the counter attack of the Schoolmen. Had he not said that it was impossible for us to discover whether or not God had arranged a mass of material and given it the power to perceive and to think? This opening wide of the doors of materialism, although materialism did not actually stalk in, led many enraged anti-Lockians to assert categorically that matter was not capable of thought.[61]

The sensationalist, Condillac, although he neither thought the soul material nor endowed matter with the capacity to think, did distinctly place primary emphasis on the faculty of feeling, and presently reduced all others to this one. By 1785 it was common academic doctrine throughout the Indies that sensation, occasioned by impressions on the sensory nerves, passed to the brain, thus becoming the basis of knowledge and the warp and woof of mental operations.[62]

[59] See above, p. 77, n. 47. AUC, *Grados en Artes,* thesis of Juan de Campos: Si sensus non haberemus, ideae nobis non essent, in Parra León, *op. cit.*, p. 92.

[60] *Ibid.*, pp. 90-95.

[61] AUC, *Grados en Artes,* thesis of Benedicto Pagés, *loc. cit.:* Materiam omnibus suis numeris absolutam et quantumvis organisatam esse cogitandi incapacem.

[62] AGG, A1., 3-12, 12797, 1924: *Assertiones philosophiae mentis, et sensuum mechanicae, ad usus physicos accomodatae: atque aliae physico-theologiae juxta mentem recentiorum Propugnandae* (Guatemala, 1785), p. 7: Sensibile dicitur illud, quod, qua tale formaliter, externorum sensuum organa immutare ea ratione potest, ut illius notio, seu perceptio passionem ipsam externi sensorii in anima consequatur. *Ibid.*, p. 20: Ex cerebro ii nervi ortum suum habent, qui spontaneis motibus peragendis, destinati sunt, ex cerebello oriuntur, qui functionibus imperio animae minime subjectis

The spiritual alone could feel, a fact which led the Condillac exponents to refute the Cartesian allegation that brutes were mere *automata*.[63] Instead, beasts were given a non-material if not spiritual mind (as the most rudimentary experience seemed to dictate), the capacity for feeling and knowing,[64] but simple brute apprehension was not regarded as a phenomenon of understanding.

One cause of the glib disparagement of Hispanic colonial culture, a cause having a much less solid basis than others, is the assumption that a philosopher was unknown when his works were only found unacceptable. By such a tenet most of the philosophers were long unknown in Europe. Such has been the case with Baruch Spinoza (1632-1677). His so-called pantheism, his conception of the universe and nature required him to insist that the love of an all-pervading God, or nature's exercise of the law of

inserviunt. *Ibid.*, 12799, 1926: *Assertiones philosophiae mentis, et sensuum mechanicae . . .*, *D.D. Franciscus de Fuentes has universiae philosophiae theses . . .* (Guatemala, 1788), p. 15: Sensatio non sit in ea corporis parte, quae a re sensibili immutatur, sed tantum in cerebro . . . . Ex cerebro ii nervi ortum suum habent, qui spontaneis motibus peragendis, destinti sunt; ex cerebello oriuntur, qui functionibus imperio animae subjectis inserviunt.

[63] *Ibid.*, Belluis nulla inest cognitio, qua in suis motibus dirigantur: omnes enim suas operationes perficiunt vi solius mechanismi. *Ibid.*, 12816, 1929, thesis of José Raymundo, 8 July, 1796: Nulla est in belluis anima spiritualis, cogitans, et sentiens.

[64] AUC, *Grados en Artes*, thesis of Teodoro Monasterios: Bruta anima gaudent sentiente et excogitante. *Ibid.*, Joaquín Hernández: Simplex apprehensio non est operatio sed passio intellectus. Parra León, *op. cit.*, p. 101. AGN, *Libro de Gobierno, desde 1796 hasta 1800*, thesis of José Suárez, 24 July, 1798: Brutorum anima non est materialis. AGG, A1, 3-12, 12817, 1930, thesis of Pablo Rivas, 1797: Bruta animantia non sunt machinae, sed praedita sunt anima sensitiva.

self-preservation, made man a part of His own substance—a part of His infinite love for Himself. It had seemed in Europe, and the opinion was universally acclaimed in America, that individuality, so dear to the Schoolmen, was lost among these particles of God. Raimundo Ruiz was but an echo of a wave of opinion in three viceroyalties when he maintained: *Anima non est particula substantiae Diviniae.*[65] Knowledge of Spinoza was common, but familiarity always produced more bitterness than understanding.[66] Not once, apparently, in the eighteenth century was there an ardent defender of this last of "the Hebrew prophets." Impious philosophers have long gleefully inquired if God could make a stone so large He Himself could not remove it. Spinoza preferred irreverence to an impasse. Substance, of which the universe is formed, and of which God Himself was part, could not be changed. The Americans did not desire to make God whimsical, wherefore they found themselves combating with Spinoza-like doctrine the Cartesian thesis that God can change the essence of His own work. "God," they said, "cannot be con-

[65] AGN, *Libro de Gobierno, desde 1796 hasta 1800,* thesis of Raimundo Ruiz, 31 July, 1799.

[66] AGG, A1., 3-12, 12830, 1934, a pamphlet, *Theses ex universa philosophia quas D. Joannes Firminus de Ayzinena et Piñol ad bachalaureatum ascendens defendebat* . . . (Guatemalae, 1806), p. 19, an especially reactionary document, includes this on Spinoza: Mascule Benedictus Spinosa (maledictum Potius appellares) Vapulet a nobis, Pantheistarumque reliquae pestes, omniumque asserta de Pantheismo, contradictionis, absurditatis, & dementiae caracteres in sese refundere sustinemus: similiter pro viribus, & impetimus atheistas, universosque mundum casu excursione materiae fortuita, crtum esse ariolantes.

nected with the possibility of possible things nor the impossibility of impossible things." *Intrinseca rerum possibilitas est a voluntate Divina omnino independens.*[67]

What did this imposing philosophical activity betoken? A generation which could favorably appraise methodical doubt and Cartesian mechanism with detachment and discuss seriously the Lockian hypothesis of a thinking material was making intellectual strides. And the change was not isolated. In the University of Mérida, high in the Venezuelan Andes, as well as in the University of San Carlos de Guatemala, and the universities of Caracas, Mexico, and Lima the revolution was thoroughly achieved in the last half of the eighteenth century.

But in the excitement of transferring from a purely authoritative system to one of doubt and experiment, it would have been surprising if the moderns had not plunged into excesses and developed and set up the new authority in place of the old.[68]

[67] AGN, *Libro de Gobierno, desde 1784 hasta 1792*, thesis of Fulgencio Ortiz, 1787: Errat Cartesius asserendo essentias rerum posse a deo mutari. Nec proinde deus conectitur cum possibilitate possibilium aut impossibilium impossibilitate. *Ibid.*, 1793-1795, thesis of Emanuel Otero, 9 February, 1794: Possibilitas rerum intrinseca a voluntate divina nullatenus pendet. *Ibid.*, thesis of Julián Castellanos, 22 January, 1793, quoted above. *Ibid.*, 1779-1784, XXIII, thesis of José Joaquín Avilés, 10 May, 1782: Dicimus implicari contradictionem, quod idem numero corpus possit bilocari circumscriptive, unde nec per absolutam Dei potentiam id fieri posse stabilimus.

[68] In the case of Archbishop "Lugdunensis's" *Instituciones filosóficas* and particularly Teodoro Almeida's *Recreación filosófica ó Diálogo sobre la filosofía natural,* used extensively in the University of Guatemala, such solidification in the new mold did take place in part.

Thus without the opposition of the traditionalists and the disagreement of modernists, the philosophical revolution might easily have resulted only in another brand of authority which, in a static condition, would have been no whit superior to that of the Prince of Philosophers and the Angelic Doctor. After all, the conservatives performed a useful service in checking the excesses against Aristotle. So, recognizing what was good in Aristotle, they laughed, even as you and I laugh, at Descartes' poor pineal gland, but the members of the new school, by accepting his methodical doubt, made a declaration of intellectual freedom—not the kind the state condones or suppresses, but the invincible kind the mind confers upon itself.

The truth is that instead of having a cultural lag of three hundred years behind Europe there was an hiatus in the Spanish colonies of approximately one generation from European innovator to American academician. Even the case for the general and constant lag of one generation between the backward universities of Europe and the quiescent ones of America, however, cannot be successfully made out as the year 1800 approached. As the eighteenth century passed, the gap became less and less. It was eighty-five years after the death of Descartes before Cartesianism began to be taught openly in the New World, but Newton was an accepted institution a half-century after the publication of his *Principia Mathematica* and almost within a decade of his death. The work of Jean Baptiste Lamarck—pointing as it did to evolution—on the origin, progress, and destruction of bodies was published in 1802 and was the subject of academic speculation in America the next year. Between 1780 and 1800, with fair allowances for transportation and isolation, the lag ceased to exist.

And for those who require economic and political justification for an intellectual transition, it was precisely on the battlefields where the most retrogressive principles of the Schoolmen had been vanquished—at Chuquisaca, Caracas, San Carlos de Lima—that the revolutionary leaders were trained. They were not a curious self-taught race, as they must have been for detractors like Baralt and Rivera to be correct. Instead, they remembered their education with gratitude. What did they know of universities, you say? One of them knew enough to dismiss the inferior Yale library contemptuously as "nothing special," and to scorn her trifling equipment as "bagatelles."

Anyone examining the records of the South American wars of independence will be amazed at the critical acumen and philosophical audacity of Sánchez Carrión, Antonio Nariño, Mariano Moreno, Bernardo Monteagudo, Andrés Bello, José Joaquín Olmedo, and Hipólito Unánue. They were not leaders who sprang full-educated from the brow of Zeus. They were the fruits of an educational discipline which was thoroughly scholastic, although it was in a free society that their mature intellects unfolded. Suppose that Pedro Peralta Barnuevo, after preparing himself for the typical encyclopedic intellectual life, had had the book of modern philosophy thrust into his hands and been pushed out into the world! One of the most distinguished careers in cultural history would not have been an unreasonable expectation. If the experience of this generation means anything, a scholastic discipline—which we laymen sometimes loosely call Jesuit methods—ultimately combined with the liberal experimental approach in a non-scholastic society, is an ideal formula for collegiate education.

It has long been the custom of specialists to assume that the theoretical foundation of the revolt against Spain rested solely upon the ideas of the French political doctrinaires of 1789. A man dropping from Mars to investigate that subject, with all second-hand treatises destroyed and forced to use original papers exclusively, would perhaps not regard the names of Rousseau, Voltaire, Montesquieu, or even Raynal as significant enough to emphasize in the book which his association with earthly university professors would force him to write. No doubt these last gave the late colonial period a definite slant, but the names which would seem of transcendant importance in this hypothetical book would be, instead, St. Thomas Aquinas, Descartes, Newton, Condillac, Pierre Gassendi, and Malebranche. Without them Raynal, Condorcet, Diderot, Benjamin Franklin, and Thomas Paine would scarcely have been heard and certainly not understood. An intellectual revolution in America involving these men was the only one consistent with the rôle of the church in the national period, and such alone could explain the surprising political conservatism of men like Unánue, Monteagudo, and even Bolívar. This intellectual revolution took place within bounds, hence the bitterness against Aristotle who, as a pagan, was out of bounds. Descartes and Condillac made their greatest mistakes, despite their vaunted freedom, in an effort to stay in bounds—in far-fetched attempts to reconcile their systems with fundamental philosophical and theological conceptions of the past. The same desire to embrace the new with little corresponding sacrifice of their heritage marked the Americans as clearly as it did Descartes. Hence Cartesianism and natural law seem scarcely more than advanced stages of scholasticism.

A picture of this transition would be too tedious to be spectacular. And it would show not an harassed doctor tacking his books in the bottom of the chairs to get an occasional glance in safety, but instead it would represent an uninterrupted perusal of the treatises of good-natured eclectics. But the new material, upon which this difference of interpretation is based, must be used with caution and with no unheedful desire to rush to the other extreme which has characterized the impugners of the black legend since Julián Juderías published his notable polemic.[69] The old explanation smacked of an hypothesis born out of a want of complete information. The result of the study of the new data, if handled properly, will be considerable, if not actually revolutionary in scope.

[69] *La leyenda negra*. Barcelona, 1912.

Yet even this revolution against the Schoolmen—to my mind the only fundamental one—had to continue its fight for its new-gained position. Even so late as the nineteenth century there were those academic Quixotes who, under the very shadow of the liberalized university, insisted as in Venezuela that the sky was a great solid canopy and that the planets passed through its portholes in their periodical movements.[70] In the last two decades of the eighteenth century in Mexico there raged a prolonged and comically serious disputation between Thomists and Scotists.[71] In 1816 they were still qualifying the law of universal attraction in Guatemala.[72] The very hopelessness of their situation had forced the Schoolmen from intransigency to obscurantism where they made their last stand.

[70] J. de Méndez y Mendoza, *Historia de la Universidad Central de Venezuela* (2 vols., Caracas, 1911-1924), I, 166-167.

[71] See AGN, *Libro de Gobierno de la Real y Pontificia Universidad de México*, XXIV.

[72] AGG, A1., 3-12, 12830, 1934: *Theses ex universa philosophia quas D. Joannes Firminus de Ayzinena et Piñol ad bachalaureatum ascendens defendebat* . . . . Quia universalem Newtonianam attractionem fabularum loco habemus; non continuo sistematico humore liniti, naturae legibus, & oculorum testimonio refragramur: illam libentissime admittimus in magnete, in succino, in Sole, in methalis, in salibus, in corporibus electricis, in fluidis, & tandem si placet, etiam in plantis.

MEDICINE

Chapter IV

THE PREFACE TO MODERN MEDICINE

The weight of authority bore down heavily upon medicine until long after substantial progress had been made in sciences of no such immediate importance to the well-being of man. This retardation of medical culture was largely the result of the prolonged victory of conservative forces over those of change with which they are ever at battle.

It was doubly tragic in the case of the Hispanic World, for in the flush of intellectual excitement after the discovery of America, Spain had not only produced a prophet of international justice in Francisco de Vitoria, but a herald of medical experiment in Gómez Pereira who distinguished the middle of the *Siglo de Oro* with a work on medical principles and facts experimentally arrived at,[1] and was happy because in that work he had added a page to the book of nature. In the opinion of the celebrated critic, Menéndez y Pelayo, he strained the very chains of Galenism.[2] Nor did Pereira stand alone. Luis Mercado attacked Hippocrates as unsuited to the modern world. Francisco Valles, "the Divine," not only gave Philip II a hot milk bath for his gout which en-

[1] *Novae Veraeque Medicinae experimentis et evidentibus rationibus comprobatae per Gometium Pereiram Medicum.* Medina del Campo, 1588.

[2] Marcelino Menéndez y Pelayo, *La ciencia española* (2 vols., Madrid, 1933), I, 402 *et seq.*

chantingly relieved the monarch, but later administered a purgative to the same potentate on the fifth day of a typhoid fever in scandalous violation of the sacred principle of the Roman Galen that the patient who grew worse on the fourth day of an illness would inevitably die on the sixth.[3] This latter achievement carried the Spanish *médico* to the pinnacle of medical fame in Spain and the Indies. And in the sense that the Norsemen discovered America before Columbus, so Reina de Zamora is reputed to have discovered the circulation of the blood before Harvey.

But Spain did not advance immediately in the realm of medicine. Nor indeed did the rest of the world. If progress were lacking in Europe, certainly the intense activity of the conquest in America rendered it even more unlikely in the Indies. Stout old Bernal Díaz del Castillo, who followed Cortés in his Xenophon-like conquest of Mexico, blithely recorded the lusty remedy used after the famous battle with the Tlascalans: "We halted for the night near a brook, and dressed our wounds on the grease we took from a dead Indian who was left on the field."[4] The conqueror thought more on how to kill than how to live. He took, therefore, little stock in drugs and doctors. To his direct mind therapeutical methods which saved life and produced results were better

[3] Quis in quarto ad pejorem statum recidunt, plerique sesto moriuntur. B. Vicuña Mackenna, *Los médicos de antaño en el Reino de Chile* (Santiago de Chile, 1877), p. 44.

[4] *True history of the conquest of Mexico* (2 vols., London, 1928), I, 122.

than the finished aphorisms of the medical classics which left the patient cold in death. Physicians were produced by the emergencies. Pizarro's wounded men accepted the services of self-constituted practitioners like the Greek, Pedro de Candia. Pedro de Valdivia, bringing everything to Chile from padres to chickens, yet brought no doctor,[5] but his woman, Inez Suárez, became the practitioner celebrated in song and story.[6]

Few conquerors succumbed in bed. Of all the companions of Pizarro only one (Mansio Sierra de Leguizama) died of disease or old age. It was violence that terminated their existence. Men so imbued with hope as were the conquistadores never faced the risk of paralyzing reflection on sickness and disaster capable of arresting their march. At the door of everlasting night it was the doctor of the soul and not of the mortal body of which the Castilian sons of a crusading century bethought themselves. The absence of the Latin physician went unnoticed and unlamented, but the priest was always present. Ever near and constraining the angry piety of Cortés before the heathen idols was Father Bartolomé Olmedo. Foremost in the fray at Inca Caxamarca was Fray Vincente de Valverde. Brought by the Araucanians to offer up his soul at Tucapel, Valdivia did so at the feet of Father Pozo whom the pagans also dispatched without the slightest sense of blasphemy.

It has been suggested that the conqueror failed to

[5] Vicuña Mackenna, *op. cit*, pp. 9-10.

[6] Stella Burke May, *The Conqueror's Lady Inés de Suárez* (New York, 1930), *passim.*

probe to the bottom of the indigene's medical knowledge. Perhaps, but the methods of the natives rarely shocked him, for they were essentially those of the Spaniards with the difference that the medicine man was unconcerned with the *Prognostics* of Hippocrates.

It has never been contended that surgery among the American Indians reached a point to excite wonder save among the Incas of Peru. Among these, the common use of slings, *bolas,* and clubs in the armies caused many a dangerous brain hernia. The discovery of once-fractured skulls where the bone has overgrown and encompassed edges of shell or silver plates indicates that the Inca surgeon saved the life of his patient. Since there is no unimpeachable evidence of the existence of the trepanning instrument known to modern surgery, one may assume that large pieces of bone were removed, long slits made, and strips of bone pried out with some obsidian, copper, or silver-tin tool. Some critics have gone so far as to say that the skill required for this dangerous operation might have been acquired in *post mortem* examinations, but skulls discovered with no indications of healing, far from indicating experiment upon cadavers as Dr. Hrdlička thinks, probably suggest that the patient died. Although it is hard to imagine an operation at the very fount of pain which could be performed successfully without the use of anesthetics, it does not follow that the Indian surgeon was familiar with this usage. It requires little imagination, on the other hand, to believe that the patient, if conscious, drugged himself with coca leaves, for this herb had long been slipping from the control of the priests and aristocrats into the hands of the comman man.[7] It is likewise dangerous to assert, as some suggest, that the Incas cauterized or washed wounds with a lotion from willow bark or used scrapings from tanned hides to stop hemorrhages. The instances upon which the case rests are too fragmentary to prove that the Incas had a significant advanced surgery.[8] The alleged facts are too uncertain to justify the charge that the busy conquerors were negligent. What we know there was to learn of medicine among the natives the Spaniards learned.

Certain diseases, which devastated the Indian population after the arrival of the Iberians, such as tuberculosis, rickets, measles, smallpox, and cholera, had never been known to the Indians, and cancer was exceptional. Otherwise Rousseau's noble savages suffered from most of the specific ills which have long laid man low. Among these even syphilis may be included, for it can no longer be confidently maintained that this disease was not there already.[9] The Que-

[7] Antonio Calancha, *Crónica Moralizada de la Provincia del Perú* (Barcelona, 1639), p. 60; José de la Acosta, *Historia Natural y Moral de Indias* (2 vols., Seville, 1590), lib. IV, cap. 22; Hipólito Unánue, "Disertación sobre el aspecto, cultivo, comercio, y virtudes de la famosa planta del Perú nombrada coca," *Mercurio Peruano*, V (9 vols., Lima, 1861-1864), 253-297.

[8] Manuel Antonio Muniz and W. J. McGee, *Primitive Trephining in Peru, Sixteenth Annual Report of the Bureau of American Ethnology, 1894-1895*, pp. 1-72; Antonio Lorena, "La medicina i la tripanación incana [*sic*], *Revista Universitaria del Cuzco*, Año IX (1920), No. 32, pp. 35-48.

[9] Vicuña Mackenna, *op. cit.*, p. 14.

chua language contained synonyms for the disease,[10] and the pathological marks on the skulls taken from the ancient Inca tombs and habitations have every sign of syphilitic ravages.[11] Modern archaeologists know, from the great number of skeletons of women and children, that deaths from childbirth and digestive ailments were also common. From all this the Spaniard could hardly be expected to have learned much, but he was so favorably disposed toward remedies and herbs used by the natives that he adopted literally hundreds now "in the pharmacopeia of the United States, such as cinchona (quinine), coca (cocaine), and cascara sagrada."[12] The padres in the mission field were all too alert for Indian drugs.[13]

Credulity led to an intermingling of medicine and superstition among the Spanish Americans which produced a medical lore as wild as the geographic.[14] Faith played so vital a part even in the practice of medicine that medical examinations in the universities in some instances were conducted in the presence of a priest.[15] The chroniclers, most of them of the so-called convent variety, sprinkled their historical

[10] Julio C. Tello, *La antigüedad de la sífilis en el Perú* (Lima, 1909), pp. 1-43. *Huanthi* was the synonym for the Spanish *bubas* (English, buboes).

[11] *Ibid.*, pp. 154-184, plates V and XV. See also pp. 189-195.

[12] Ales Hrdlička, "Advanced Surgery found among Indians," *The American Scholar*, I (1932), 374-376.

[13] The manuscripts division of the Biblioteca Nacional in Mexico City boasts some serious compilations on herbs with elaborate drawings.

[14] Juan B. Ambrosetti, *Supersticiones y leyendas* (Buenos Aires, 1917), pp. 145-160.

[15] Such a step was not regarded as suppression.

works with stories of extraordinary cures through the ministrations of herbs and occult matter as well as through the beneficence of the saints. The padres consistently worked against the practices of medicine men where they impinged upon theology, but they tended to look upon the Indian's knowledge of medicine as the natural result of his primordial experience. Indeed, the credulity of the chronicler is frequently as amazing as the remedy. One of them recorded with awe that a group of starving Indian prisoners, when reduced to desperation, cut away the calves of their legs for food and that upon the subsequent application of herbs the flesh grew back as it originally was.[16]

Remedies were numerous and strange during most of the colonial period. The emblem of indigenous medicine, the bezoar stone, taken from the intestines of certain ruminants, was supposed to have extraordinary medical properties and was considered especially efficacious as an antidote for poison and as a remedy for venereal diseases, for which purpose it was dispatched to the kings of Spain. Likewise, ground to dust, mixed with water and drunk, it was "supposed to make the heart glad." To its efficacy even Father Bernabé Cobo, among the most scientific observers of his time, paid an unequivocal tribute. The surest index of the esteem in which an article is held—the price—soared to 250 pesos in

[16] Diego Rosales, *Historia general del Reino de Chile* (ed. Vicuña Mackenna, 3 vols., Valparaiso, 1877-1878), I, 231, 240, 250. See A. Fuenzalida Grandón, *El desarrollo intelectual en Chile, 1541-1810* (Santiago, 1903), pp. 422-423.

Potosí.[17] Among the medicines found in the drug stores and hospitals of eighteenth-century Chile were counted: capon water, wild boar's teeth, calcined frogs, condor fat, balsam of gourds, crawfish eyes, claw of a tapir, unicorn, jawbones of unclean fish, lizard oil, spine of vipers, spirits of earthworms, and wing bones of vultures.[18]

Attracted, like the aborigine, by the heavens, the colonial doctors looked to the skies and to the collision of celestial bodies for an explanation of diseases, especially when they assumed the proportions of an epidemic. It was in the realm of occult medicine, where night-flowering plants, livers of the pelican, the blood of a black lamb, and gall bladder were the favorite remedies, that women came into their own. Some of these female medicasters were midwives, for women had a monopoly upon obstetrics. Men who violated the restriction were subject to rigorous punishment in the viceroyalties.

Notions of medicine in the universities, judged by views of the professors who essayed to write treatises, were, up until the medical revolution of the eighteenth century, little less bizarre than those of these medical sibyls. In 1694 Dr. Francisco Bermejo y Roldán, professor holding the leading chair of medicine in the University of San Marcos in Lima and member of the medical tribunal of the viceroyalty,

[17] Bernabé Cobo, *Historia del Nuevo Mundo* (4 vols., Seville, 1890-1893), I, 227.

[18] J. T. Medina, *Cosas de la colonia* (2 vols., Santiago de Chile, 1910), Archivo del Ministerio del Interior, vol. 966, cited in Fuenzalida, *op. cit.*, p. 136.

pronounced a discourse on measles[19] in which he clarified the ailment by describing it as an "acute, epidemical, pestilential, regional, or native disease." He graced his lecture with a classification of diseases in which he arranged them in categories of "similar, dissimilar, particular, and universal or common." When the disease was common, he felt no doubt that in contrast to other times the cause lay in the atmosphere, called by José de Contreras[20] the infernal fire of the pestilential air, which "by pulses and respirations" sustained and changed us. Malignant infections and pestilences were also the result of particular configurations and positions of the planets. About the same time (1687), when Pedro de Peralta was not long past twenty, and just approaching full intellectual maturity, he published with the sanction of the royal medical tribunal and of the viceroy himself a treatise on the *Aberrations of Nature or the Origin of Monsters*.[21] In this medico-theological treatise, Peralta, while giving a surprisingly sane physiological appraisal of the specimen, gravely recorded the birth of a creature of two heads and four arms in Lima during the preceding year. One of the important questions involved was: Do such creatures have souls and, if so, one or two? Faced with this cosmic dilemma, these men of learning decided that the bap-

[19] *Discvrso de la Enfermedad del Sarampion Experimentada en la Civdad de los Reyes del Perù*. Lima, 1694.

[20] Fuego infernal que en aires pestilentes. . . . J. T. Medina, *La imprenta en Lima* (4 vols., Santiago de Chile, 1904-1907), II, 200.

[21] *Desvíos de la Naturaleza ó del Origen de los Monstruos*. Lima, 1687.

tism of a projecting foot by the midwife was sufficient.[22] When at the end of the century José Pastor de Larrinaga,[23] respected son of San Marcos, engaged his talents in an inquiry into whether or not "a woman could be converted into a man," it was the novel, perhaps, more than the medical problem of bisexuality that caused interest.

Both before and after the acceptance of the theory of the circulation of the blood, bleeding was the uniform practice and heroic proceeding of the physician. For tuberculosis and "plethora,"[24] for digestive disorders and skin diseases the Latin physician—thus called to distinguish him from the Romance doctor *(Romancista)* who knew no Latin—always bled. And of medical treatises on the subject, such as they were, there was no lack, and in the middle of the eighteenth century medicine was still veritably buried in astrology. A book on bleeding and purgatives which appeared in Lima in 1645[25] made both treatments contingent upon the heavenly configurations,

[22] Peralta accepted this disposal of the case easily. See Pedro de Peralta, *Lima fundada* (2 parts, Lima, 1737), part II, canto VI, n. 95. Monsters long remained an obsession of those who professed and spoke the language of science. See "Metamórfosis Humanas: noticia de la extraña desfiguración de una niña," *Mercurio Peruano*, IV (1861), 70-74, 265, 301-313.

[23] See "Disertación en que se trata si una mujer se puede convertir en hombre," *Mercurio Peruano*, IX, 2-16.

[24] Bleeding prevailed in the theses as well as in the texts. AGG, A1., 3-12, 12821, 1931, thesis of José Jacobo Celiz (1800); Plethorae curatio absolvitur missu sanguinis. (P. 106, *Inst. Med.* [Boerhaave]; *ibid.*, 12827, 1933, thesis of Mariano Viscarra, 14 January, 1804: Si plethora hydropi conjungitur, missio sanguinis institui debet.

[25] Juan Jerónimo Navarro, *Sangrar y pvrgar en dias de conjvncion. . . .* Lima, 1645.

for it was an age in which not even a "light purgative was taken unless the situation of the stars was favorable."[26] Fifteen years after the publication of this treatise of 1645 there appeared in Lima another work in which much space was devoted to such problems as: "Whether the doctrines and sentences of the doctors and astrologers for the Arctic are common to both poles. . . . The nature of fevers and the planets which dominate them. . . . Judgment of illnesses caused by the moon's being in Taurus, aggravated by Saturn. . . . The diseases which originate from the sign which is in the ascendency."[27]

In view of the universal practice of bleeding, it is little wonder that Dr. Sangrado in Le Sage's *Gil Blas* seemed so plausible when he took six full cups of blood to supply "the lack of transpiration," repeated the operation in six hours, and ordered the same done the next morning, holding that it was a mistake to suppose that blood was necessary to life. Repetition of the operation based on this principle every hour or so, while the patient was gorged with hot water, placed the victim on the brink of death the second day and passed him over it on the third. There were so many causes of death, and science was so uncompromising, that the filling of the cemeteries with

[26] H. Valdizán, *La facultud de medicina en Lima* (3 vols., Lima, 1927-1929), I, 33.

[27] Juan de Figueroa, *Opvscvlo de Astrologia en Medicina, y de los Terminos, y Partes de la Astronomia Necessarias para el Vso della. . . .* Lima, 1660. Another work of the same tenor, approved by the leading professor of the University of San Marcos, was José de la Rocha y Carranza, *Calendario astromedico para el año de 1683*. Lima, 1682.

these bloodless cadavers conveyed no lesson to the medical profession of the epoch.

An Italian doctor, Federico Bottoni, a century after Harvey's celebrated discovery, wrote a pamphlet for the enlightenment of the professors and doctors of Lima entitled *Evidence of the Circulation of the Blood.*[28] On behalf of the cloister of Lima it must be said, however, that the book was no shock, for among those carried along with the argument were the medical examiner, Dr. Juan de Avendaño y Campoverde, and the scholar, Pedro Peralta Barnuevo, who found no unsound doctrine in it. Nevertheless, one Bernabé Sánchez felt disposed to debate the point with a pamphlet called a *Discourse against the Circulation of the Blood.*[29]

And the controversy over the expediency of bleeding long went on in print.[30] Students, following Galen[31] or Andrés Piquer,[32] could still deny or doubt the circulation of the blood, for an Englishman, never eager to praise a Spaniard in colonial days, reported that as late as 1787 blood was taken from the right arm one day and from the left on the next to equalize the red liquid and thus maintain the equilibrium of the patient.[33]

The evolution of anatomy and surgery is a pain-

[28] *Evidencia de la Circulacion de la Sangre* . . . . Lima, 1723. BNL, tomo 89.

[29] Bernabé Sánchez, *Discurso contra la Circulacion de la Sangre* . . . . Lima, 1723. See H. Unánue, *Obras científicas y literarias* (ed. E. Larrabure y Unánue, 3 vols., Barcelona, 1914).

[30] Juan José de Villarreal, *Satisfaccion a vna Calumnia Imaginaria, y Defensa de una Verdadera Calvmnia.* Lima, 1759.

[31] *De curandis ratione per sanguinis missionem.*

[32] Andrés Piquer, *Instituciones médicas.* Madrid, 1762.

[33] Joseph Townsend, *Journey through Spain* (3 vols., London, 1792), III, 282.

ful story, and to arraign the tardiness of the colonials without remembering that of Europe is irresistibly natural. Dissection, like scientific knowledge of the blood, was everwhere regrettably slow in arriving. There is evidence that as early as 1488 permission was given to dissect a certain number of human bodies every year at Zaragoza,[34] Spain, but the time was not ripe.

Autopsies entered the medical picture in Spanish America without fanfare and before the erection of formal amphitheatres. The enchanting and unorthodox rhymes of Juan Caviedes, late seventeenth-century poet of Peru, on anatomy in the Hospital of San Andrés in Lima mingle a progressive story of autopsies with lamentable errors of diagnosis. In Francisco Bermejo's pamphlet of 1694 on measles one learns of no less than six autopsies performed here and there in the City of Kings. Far to the north, in New Spain, Don Carlos de Sigüenza y Góngora wrote it into his will that his body should be dissected to enable the surgeons to find the cause of the disease which proved fatal (1700), as well as to relieve sufferers who might follow him. The doctors "found a stone the size of a peach-stone in his right kidney where he said that he had had pain."[35]

Naturally, the mere liberty of carving bodies was no open sesame to perfect knowledge in imperfectly

[34] Rafael Altamira, *Historia de España y de la civilización española* (4 vols., Barcelona, 1900-1911), II, 515.

[35] Irving A. Leonard, *Don Carlos de Sigüenza y Góngora* (Berkeley, 1929), p. 181. The entire testament of Sigüenza is published in Francisco Pérez Salazar, *Biografía de D. Carlos Sigüenza y Góngora . . .* (Mexico, 1928), pp. 161-192.

trained minds seeking confirmation of phenomena observed in life. Inflammation, a uniform term, was likely to be considered a cause rather than effect. Bermejo described a kidney examined in one of the Lima autopsies in typical language as "swollen, gangrened, with black . . . points and spots." One advantage of colonial pathological anatomy, however, was a relative simplicity of terminology, for while it was not considered in the best or most imposing taste to write in Romance, the practice was not forbidden and was resorted to sometimes by learned doctors through an altogether intelligible desire to make themselves understood. A kidney stone "the size of a peach-stone,"[36] a liver "larger than that of a cow," and a uterus "like a child's head" were graphic descriptions and immediately significant. However, not even the Romance language made it clear whether a "lost organ" meant one which atrophied and disappeared or one which had merely ceased to function.

Upon the establishment of the chair of method in the University of San Marcos de Lima in 1711, Viceroy Diego Ladrón de Guevara stipulated that the professor should undertake the dissection of a cadaver every week in the Hospital of San Andrés before both students and surgeons.[37] It is by no means certain that Pedro López de los Godos, the first active pro-

[36] Antonio de Robles, "Diario de Sucesos Notables," *Documentos para la historia de México*, ser. 1, III, 262, cited in Leonard, *op. cit.*, pp. 180-181.

[37] This chair, however, suffering the typical vicissitudes of an easy-going generation, was created anew in 1723 after a lapse, but was not finally confirmed until 1752.

fessor of the subject there, complied with the clause requiring him to hold anatomical demonstrations. It was of basic importance that the practice was taken for granted. Dr. Federico Bottoni called Dr. Pablo Petit, a French physician very popular in Lima, a "most excellent surgeon and anatomist."

Dr. Francisco Matute, a practical teacher of anatomy, had the distinction, and no doubt pleasure, of seeing his colleagues, whose scholastic conceptions made them admirers of prestige, accept his word with the same credulity which had made them defer formerly to the scholastic authorities. Not satisfied with mere clinical instruction, he began a course in 1770 through the actual use of cadavers and, after the manner of pioneer teachers, carried students across his very threshold for private teaching. Likewise, according to the reward of distinguished teachers, his work perhaps bore greatest fruit in one of his students, José Pastor de Larrinaga. That prolific contributor to the *Mercurio Peruano*,[38] notwithstanding some of the ridiculous bypaths he explored, was useful as a propagandist and as an audacious exemplar who was undaunted before the risks of abdominal surgery about which most of his contemporaries thought in terms of the extreme unction.

The royal amphitheatre of Lima, approved in 1753, became a reality only in 1792. By then the tone was distinctly modern, for the professor dissected the body and answered the questions formulated by the students and assistants, "except when

[38] His gropings were typical of American scientific men while theory so far exceeded discovery and knowledge.

these consisted of subtleties, or had a metaphysical character, in which case they should remain unanswered. . . ."[39] The dissection of animals may have been motivated by a desire to study comparative anatomy, but more likely was the result of the difficulty of securing human cadavers. Religious practices still threw a hush of sanctity about death which rendered it both costly and impious to use the human corpse. But economy soon triumphed over creed, for in 1809 seven of nine dissections were of human bodies, one that of a lamb, and one of a dog. A sheep now cost three pesos, a dog six reales, while the price of an inedible human body ranged between one peso four reales and one peso six reales.[40] Thus, while the cost of a human body was greater than that of a dog, it was less than that of a sheep.

Hipólito Unánue (1755-1833), Peru's greatest pioneer of modern medicine, had by this time arrived at the scene, and he conceded anatomy a place of elemental importance in medical culture. "The ignorance of anatomy before the terrible army of disease," he said to the Peruvians upon the occasion of his inaugural address in the Royal Amphitheatre of San Andrés (1792), "has ruined our cities, desolated our fields, disintegrated our mines, and the . . . hands which foment their splendor, fecundity, and riches . . . . Unfortunate Peru! This has been your lot: sunk deep in a mortal ignorance of anatomy, you

[39] See Valdizán, *op. cit.*, I, 169; II, 3-18. See also Valdizán, "Los médicos de la colonia," *Gaceta de los Hospitales* (Lima, 1911).

[40] "Relación del Disector Anatómico D. Norberto de Vaga," quoted in Valdizán, *op. cit.*, II, 111-112.

lacked intelligent doctors in your provinces, . . . diseases decimated your population. . . ."[41] The program which he prepared for the Royal (medical) College of San Fernando was regarded by the Junta of Cádiz as a curriculum more appropriate for a university. He stood for a course in zoönomia, including something of biology as a natural forerunner of practical surgery. A recommendation of obstetrical anatomy was even more revolutionary. But these two hopes are most useful as indices to Unánue's mind, for they did not then get beyond the state of projection.

Although not so significant as in Peru, progress in anatomy was made in Mexico. For example, in the year 1576 Dr. Juan de la Fuente was conducting experiments in the field. Anatomical dissections were reputed likewise to have been begun at an early date in the *Hospital Real de los Naturales.*

A foreign surgeon, Dr. José Dumont, again initiated dissections on human cadavers in the capital of New Spain around 1752. Although Francisco A. Flores supposed the novelty to have become more frequent after the establishment of the Royal School of Surgery in 1768,[42] the practice was allowed to lapse in the university at least, for we find the full cloister of the University of Mexico in 1774[43] informing the viceroy in a *consulta* to his excellency

[41] Inaugural address of H. Unánue in the Royal Amphitheatre of San Andrés, *Mercurio Peruano*, IV, 144-190, *passim.*

[42] Francisco A. Flores, *Historia de la medicina en México, desde la época de los indios hasta la presente* (3 vols., Mexico, 1886-1888), II, 264.

[43] AGN, *Libro de Claustros, desde 1771 hasta 1779.*

that the total eclipse of the useful sciences was now over. The "good subjects," the doctors said, had just been reënthroned after centuries of barbarism, and with them anatomy. The dissections hitherto provided for,[44] they said, had been allowed to fall into abeyance. The operations, when performed at all, had been made not upon human bodies, but upon those of animals. At last both rector and cloister petitioned the viceroy with vehemence to make the royal anatomical amphitheatre available when a suitable body could be obtained. A committee of professors from the University of Mexico saw to it that a candidate as "interne" performed his duties, studied properly, and attended the needy punctually and efficaciously. If so, he had "instructed himself in all that concerns the perfect physician."[45] It was now required that the medical student should spend two years in the Medical Academy. There he was subjected, however, to tests and ceremonies. An examination in theoretical and practical medicine followed a sort of forensic celebration in which the "interne" was expected to handle all comers in *materia medica* and the doctrines of Carlos Dumas.[46] During the

[44] *Constituciones de la Real y Pontificia Universidad de México*, Nos. 124 y 269 (Palafox edition).

[45] Certificate of Dr. Antonio Céspedes, 31 August, 1801, signed by the committee in charge of observation in the Hospital of San Andrés. AGN, *Libro de Gobierno de la . . . Universidad de México, desde 1795 hasta 1806.*

[46] This French writer (1765-1813) was the author of various works in anatomy, physiology, and chronic diseases. Certificates of José Ygno. Muñoz Siliceo, 6 February, 1819, and Juan Nepomuceno y Avila, 19 May, 1817. AGN, *Certificaciones de Variedad de Asuntos*, 1797-1827. AGG, A1., 3-12, 12824, 1933: Examen

years immediately before independence the necessity of anatomical studies was, therefore, thoroughly recognized in Peru and Mexico and perhaps elsewhere in the colonies. Otherwise there could have been no rigidly prescribed probationary period of observation. Mexico had her counterpart of Unánue in such men as Dr. Luis Montaña. In the years immediately preceding independence, therefore, the necessity of anatomical studies was widely recognized in America.

Anatomico-Fisiologico. El Br. D. Cyrilo Flores cursante de Medicina y Cirugia, demonstrara la fabrica del cuerpo humano en los Esqueletos y estampas anatomicas; y expondra el ingenio y uso de cada una de las partes que le componen, por los Aforismos de la *economia animal* del gran Boerhaave. University of San Carlos, 2 May, 1803.

Chapter V

PUBLIC HEALTH AND THE MODERNIZATION OF MEDICAL INSTRUCTION

I

Spanish medicine was so highly developed politically as to anticipate much that has been done in the realm of public health in the twentieth century. Science only needed complementary development. In fact, even before the sixteenth century, quacks and malpractice were often enough recognized as such to warrant stringent regulations in Castile. Taking note of the great prevalence of charlatanry, Charles V applied the laws of Castile to America in 1535 and forbade certain classes of persons to be physicians, surgeons, and druggists in the Indies. Indeed, no one who was not a graduate of an approved university and duly examined could arrogate the title of bachelor, doctor, or master after 1621.[1] Before the formal creation of the *protomedicato*, the viceroy of New Spain and the presidents and governors of the other American colonies were required to have the drug stores visited and all bad medicines destroyed and the owners punished in accordance with the harm wrought by their wares.[2]

The creation of the office of *protomedicato*[3] in

[1] *Recopilación de las Leyes de los Reinos de las Indias*, lib. V, tít. vi, leyes 5 (1535), 4 (1621, 1648).

[2] *Ibid.*, ley 7 (1538).

[3] A tribunal of surgery was created in Peru by 1804.

America (1570) was a signal step in the direction of the control of medical practice. Previously the work of this body had been done by the *cabildo* or town council as, no doubt, remained the case in small places.[4]

Philip II, while naming the general physicians to govern the medical profession in the New World, issued the first extensive instruction in 1570. The necessity and desire of preserving his subjects "in a long life" and "in perfect health," which had already led to the establishment of chairs of medicine in the Indies, now constrained him to send his royal physicians.

In general terms the *protomédico* was to be a field observer of science—a naturalist—in order to promote the knowledge and well-being of the little-known Americas. From all surgeons, doctors, old settlers, and anyone else who might know or have something on the subject, he collected data and made reports on herbs, trees, plants, and medicinal seeds, as well as the use and quantity of the medicaments, methods of growing them, information on the species, and whether they grew in dry or humid climate. The *protomédico* was expected also to make reports and to send to Spain specimens of all medicinal plants not already delivered to the mother country. Out of such an investigation Philip II required and expected a good natural history to develop which, in the case of Mexico, was a desire that did not go unrequited.[5]

[4] Valdizán, *op. cit.*, I, 21.

[5] Francisco de Fernández (who, in this respect after his appointment in 1571, at least exercised the functions of the medical ex-

It was specified that the *protomédico* should reside in a city with an *audiencia* and chancellery and exercise a jurisdiction extending five leagues from the city. Beyond that point he could not be expected to make calls, yet he could examine candidates for medical practice from outlying districts even when there were physicians there qualified to give the required examinations, provided the applicants presented themselves in the city of his residence. Regular local public physicians lost their jurisdiction when the *protomédico* was in the vicinity. The fees placed upon examinations and licenses were fixed by this medical officer in collaboration with the royal *audiencia.* The public physician (*protomédico*) meted out punishment to violators of the law in the medical realm, but he lacked the power to do so unless sanctioned by some judicial authority ranging in importance from president of the *audiencia* (who was the first choice) to the ordinary justice of the peace. He could not exercise his prerogatives, moreover, before presenting his credentials to the president and *oidores* of the *audiencia.*[6] The most obvious task of these men, the examining and licensing of candidates for the medical professions, was amplified in 1579 when the crown required that no physician, surgeon, druggist, barber, or bone-setter could be licensed without a personal appearance before the *protomédico* and compliance with the laws and standards of the kingdom.

aminer). AGN, *Libro de Claustros, desde 1779 hasta 1788*, claustro de 13 de julio de 1786.

[6] *Recopilación . . . de las Indias*, lib. V, tít. vi, leyes 1 and 6.

The establishment, by special, royal *cédula,* of the *Tribunal del Protomedicato General del Reyno* was merely the culmination of this unique movement of medical control. There is, for example, adequate evidence of the presence of active *protomédicos* in Guatemala before the creation of the formal tribunal there in 1793 with Dr. José Felipe Flores, professor of medicine in the University of San Carlos, as presiding officer. On February 6, 1777, the *protomedicato* of Lima named Antonio Corbella as "*Theniente-Proto-Medico*" of Buenos Aires, Tucumán, and Paraguay—many months before Viceroy Vértiz, acting upon a royal dispatch of May 3, 1778, appointed Dr. Miguel Gorman to the troubled post of "*Protomedico General.*"[7] A *protomédico,* therefore, no more bespeaks a *protomedicato* than an *oidor* signifies an *audiencia.*

Generally, but not always, located in the viceregal capitals, this *protomedicato* became a tribunal of justice, and one of the four or five most important corporations in the Indies. It began in a fashion humble enough, even in the City of Kings, for in 1569, the

[7] Unfortunately the archive of the *protomedicato* in Guatemala was burned in a medical-school fire in Guatemala City in 1923. Dr. Francisco Asturias, who, in the preparation of his *Historia de la medicina en Guatemala* (Guatemala, 1902), used the archive extensively, altogether neglected to support what he wrote by formal references. See *Real cédula,* Aranjuez, 21 de Junio de 1793, Carlos Martínez Durán, *Síntesis de la medicina colonial en Guatemala* (Guatemala, 1936), pp. 22-23. See also Archivo Colonial de Guatemala, *Autos sobre erección de Protomedicato.* For the documentation on the *protomedicato* in Buenos Aires, see Juan Ramón Beltrán, *Historia del Protomedicato de Buenos Aires.* Buenos Aires, 1937. This work is more a compilation of documents than a monograph or analysis.

first year of the government of the ever-memorable and itinerant Francisco de Toledo, Dr. Antonio Sánchez, who had been invested with the title of medical examiner in Madrid in 1568, and who had accompanied the viceroy to Peru, assumed the office on the terms offered to the first medical examiner of South America in 1538.

It was in the great capitals that the *Protomedicato General* as a court and board of medical examiners assumed functions of considerable importance exercised at various times with varying degrees of zeal. As early as January, 1527, *protomédicos* took the oath of office in New Spain.[8] From a single person the office developed, certainly before 1585, into a board, thus heralding the dawn of the supreme medical tribunal. The presiding officer, now named by the viceroy, held office as "*protomédico general de toda esta nueva españa.*" In 1646 the world was given another indication of the genuine desire for a high type of civil service when it was proclaimed through a royal *cédula* that the professor of *prima* (first chair) of medicine should always be the presiding officer of the *protomedicato* with the other members subject to royal appointment.[9] Moreover, the body over which he thus presided could direct the medical profession through the exercise of the censorship of medical books.[10]

[8] *Actas de Cabildo de la Ciudad de México* (Mexico, 1889), lib. I, p. 115. Fernando Ocaranza, *Historia de la medicina en México* (Mexico, 1934), p. 127.

[9] Real cédula de 18 de febrero de 1646. *Colección de reales cédulas sobre la Universidad de México.* See Flores, *op. cit.*, II, 167-187.

[10] See the approval of Bottoni, *op. cit.*, above.

Notwithstanding these seemingly extensive precautions charlatanry flourished. But the Spaniard, refusing to accept the verdict of a single generation, repeated legislation from time to time which had not worked for centuries. The regular Latin doctors evinced zeal for the public welfare, for they were ever exercised about the practice of the quack, perhaps with one eye on his gains and the other on his injury to society. Professors of the faculty of medicine of the University of San Marcos de Lima, for example, took advantage of the Royal *Protomedicato* to hale their Romance rivals before its stern justice.[11] And with the passing of the eighteenth century and the dawn of the nineteenth the tribunal, with scientifically disposed doctors in control, became a watchdog of the profession and so powerful as to abash political officials of some importance. So low, moreover, had the supernatural fallen in the realm of medicine that the *protomédico* of Peru ordered all copies of the long and unauthorized work on miraculous cures, written by the religious medicaster Father Confides, collected and burned in the public square. Under the driving conviction of Dr. Miguel Tafur, the tribunal, in the somewhat confused days on the eve of independence, was maintained with growing

[11] BNL, *Papeles varios del Perú*, pp. 89-91. *Causa medico-criminal que, en este Real Protomedicato del Perù, han seguido los Professores de la Facultad Mèdica contra los Cirujanos, Pharmaceùticos, Phlebotómicos &c . . . Y Oracion conminatoria, que el dia 4 de Octubre de 1764 dixo sobre el assunto uno de los Conjueces de aquel Tribunal, presidido entonces por el Doct. D. Hipólito Bueno de la Rosa, Catedrático de Prima de Medicina en la Real Universidad de San Marcos, y Protomédico General de los Reynos del Perú, confirmado por su Magestad.* Lima, 1764.

strength and prestige. The president or governor of Cuzco, appointing a lieutenant medical examiner on January 4, 1816, was soon corrected for his presumption. But concern for public health also dictated energetic measures against the almost inconceivable blatancy of the numerous fake practitioners. On February 5, 1816, the medical examiner denied a license to Santiago Ogle who, pretending to be a professor of medicine and surgery from Edinburgh, presented in sole proof of his claim a paper with neither signature nor seals. A religious, Fray Sebastián Fernández, who pretended to exercise the profession of medicine merely because two friends testified they had "seen him cure," was denied a license.[12]

The problem with which these medical officials and tribunals were grappling went far beyond the suppression of superstitious literature and quack doctors. These men were also the guardians of the public health. And in playing that rôle they could hardly have been opposed by more numerous or more cosmic obstacles. Tidal waves, earthquakes, tropical pestilences, and ordinary contagious diseases common to man everywhere, rarely waited for the population to recover before striking again with a new disease if the old had run itself out of epidemic proportions. A strange epidemic appearing in Chile in 1730 was known as "ball of fire" by virtue of having appeared simultaneously with a meteor.

Sanitary conditions, with which there was not enough scientific knowledge to cope, were horrible

[12] Papers concerning the case in Archivo de la Facultad de Medicina, libros 1816 á 1819. See Valdizán, *op. cit.*, III, 143.

to the point of nausea in mortals whose sensibilities were, it must be remembered, not fastidious. Towns and cities in and out of the tropics reeked with filth. Streets went for months at a time without being swept. But as nature guides a blind bat around a tree, so man's nose guides him around that which stinks regardless of whether decaying matter is considered hygienic or not. So late as 1796 we find a member of the cloister of the University of Mexico protesting that the populace should be prevented from relieving themselves with complete abandon in the Zócalo, the central plaza.[13]

In view of the sanitary conditions throughout the colonies, it comes as no surprise that some part of Peru was visited on an average of every four years between 1525 and 1825 by epidemics of smallpox, measles, syphilis, typhoid fever, itch, dysentery, diphtheria, bubonic plague, yellow fever, rabies, whooping cough, which took from 200,000 lives down at each blow.[14] And there was a horror of the dead bodies which ended not until the very bricks of the death chamber had been pulled out. Officials not reporting deaths were fined heavily. Sacristans in the churches, finding them overflowing, piled the bodies outside in the streets. During certain ravages in 1771 and 1793 time could only be found to cross the arms of the dead upon their breasts. Of hands to bury the victims there were none; both disease and mental

[13] AGN, *Libro de Gobierno, desde 1782 hasta 1812*, Pedro Basave to Dr. José Vicente Sánchez, June, 1796.

[14] José Toribio Polo, *Apuntes sobre las epidemias en el Perú*, pp. 3-43; *ibid., Revista Histórica*, V (1913), 50-90.

shock rendered the populace inert. First recourse was had to "the most holy Virgin." Thereafter, recourse was had to agencies more purely human.

Smallpox was perhaps the worst affliction of New Spain. Imported from Spain in 1520, it carried off, according to some authorities, half the population of Mexico during the century. Four epidemics between 1537 and 1546 dispatched eight hundred thousand indigenes. Another of great proportions in 1555 was followed in 1576 by a disastrous run of the disease which accounted for upwards of two million mortals between Mexico and Oaxaca. The ravages continued into the eighteenth century, and it was 1797 before active scientific discoveries were being used in Mexico to combat this pestilence.[15]

The scientific attack on smallpox was sporadic in America, but unbounded interest in the question led most men with medical education, and some without it, to write about and to practice inoculation (transferring the virus from a person suffering with the disease to one without it in order to give a light preventative case) and vaccination. Although it is claimed inoculation was practiced in America as early as 1722,[16] it seems that the Chilean-educated doctor, Friar Matías del Carmen Verdugo, had some claim to the distinction of first inoculating for the disease in the Spanish colonies (1765). In the bitter epidemics of 1765 and 1774, a professor in the University of San Felipe, Pedro Manuel de Chaparro, proceeded

[15] Flores, *op. cit.*, II, 214.

[16] P. Dignat, *Histoire de la médecine et des médecins à travers les âges* (Paris, 1899), p. 218.

to work by a process of direct inoculation; that is, by passing the virus from the victim to a perfectly well person. Of more than 500 persons thus inoculated in Santiago in 1774 none died, although a third of the patients with the disease had died in the epidemic of 1765.[17] As a result of this success Chaparro's crude needle continued through the succeeding epidemics of 1785 and 1789.

The practice did not spread, however, from a single focal point in America. Domingo de Soria suggested in the 1770's that inoculation be put into practice in Lima, and in 1778 a formal opinion was prepared and printed by the progressive Dr. Cosme Bueno.[18] Condamine's memorandum on inoculation was translated and circulated in Guatemala in 1780.[19] A pamphlet published in Madrid on smallpox and contagion in 1784 led the doctors to agitate for the isolation of the affected, the burning of sulphur, and the sprinkling of rooms with vinegar.[20]

A perfect illustration of the type of literature some

[17] José Pérez García, *Historia natural, militar, civil, y sagrada del Reino de Chile* (2 vols., Santiago, 1900), II, 387.

[18] *Parecer que dió el doctor don Cosme Bueno sobre la representación que hace el padre fray Domingo de Soria para poner en pràctica la inoculación de las viruelas.* Lima, 1778.

[19] Manuel González Batres, *Methodo de la inoculacion de las viruelas que reviere M. de la Condaminé en su celebre Memoria, sobre dicha Inoculacion leida en la Asemblea publica de la Academia Real de Ciencias de Paris el 24 de Abril de 1754, traducida del Idioma Frances al Castellano por Don Manuel Gonzales de Batres, quien lo da a la prensa a beneficio público.* Nueva Guatemala, 1780.

[20] Francisco Gil, *Disertación físico-médica, el la qual se prescribe un método seguro para preservar a los pueblos de viruelas, hasta lograr la completa extinción de ellas en todo el reyno.* Madrid, 1784; *ibid.*, 1796.

years later (1815) was the work of Dr. Narciso Esparragoza, of the cloister of the University of Guatemala, who, when petitioned by the *ayuntamiento,* responded with a pamphlet on the control of smallpox which, in contrast to the pompous impotence of preceding surgeons, revealed a good grasp of the problem of contagion.[21] Esparragoza recommended twelve precautions to prevent the spread of smallpox. At the top of the list he placed the exclusion of all persons and merchandise from afflicted cities. He enjoined them to keep such necessary provisions and clothes as had to be imported in quarantine for fifteen days while they were well aired and smoked with sulphur. Isolation of the early cases should be made even if the precaution necessitated caring for the poor involved at public expense. Guards should be stationed to keep the approaches to the city closed. The dead, it was ordered, should not repose in the churches or thickly populated centers but in the open country. The clothes of the victims were to be boiled with lye and all letters to be smoked and "cleaned with vinegar." Neither infants at the breast nor the sick were to be spared vaccination, results of which should be looked for on the seventh or eighth day.

The new technique of immunization made known

[21] Biblioteca Nacional de Guatemala, *Discursos,* I, No. 7: Dr. Narciso Esparragoza, Protomédico y cirujano de Camara Honorario de S. M., Methodo sencillo y facil para el conocimiento y curacion de las viruelas. A solicitud del Excmo. Ayuntamiento de esta capital en obsequio y beneficio de la humanidad . . . . Nueva Guatemala, 1815. A similar case is Dr. Luis Montaña, *Instruccion para ministrar la vacuna.* Mexico, 1815.

by Edward Jenner in 1798 was soon fully incorporated. Already the incredulous were beginning to be vaccinated by force. But direct inoculation was now prohibited by the royal decree on vaccination.[22] One pioneer of inoculation, Fray Pedro Manuel Chaparro, had the distinction of administering the first vaccine virus, brought across the mountains from Buenos Aires in 1805, three years before the great Spanish health expedition of Manuel Julián Grijales reached Santiago.[23]

Activity in relation to the subject was incessant. Jenner's work on cows and smallpox virus was published in Lima in 1802,[24] and a summary of the origin and discovery of vaccine, written originally in French, made its appearance in Lima in the same year.[25] The periodicals of Europe were scanned in the search for improvements in vaccination to be adapted "to the simplicity of the indigenes."[26]

The attitude of the Spanish government was likewise far from academic. The minister of the king's possession beyond the seas, in the name of King Charles IV, signed a circular in 1803 calling attention to a medical expedition, under the direction of

[22] Esparragoza, *op. cit.*, p. 17.

[23] Fuenzalida, *op. cit.*, pp. 452-454.

[24] *Extracta acerca del origen y efectos de una enfermedad conocida con el nombre de viruelas de las vacas, por Eduardo Jenner. Impreso en Londres en 1798, traducido del inglés y reimpreso en Lima por Guillermo del Rio.* Año de 1802.

[25] *Origen y descubrimiento de la vacuna. Traducido del francés por Don Pedro Hernández, médico del real colegio &c. Impreso en Madrid y reimpreso en Lima por Guillermo del Rio.* Año de 1802.

[26] Biblioteca Nacional de Guatemala, *Discursos*, I, No. 15: *Cartilla de vacunar.* Guatemala, 1829.

Francisco Xavier Balmis, which was to visit America, for general vaccination.[27] Upon setting sail from Coruña in 1803 some boys who had never had the smallpox were taken aboard so that, vaccinated successively on the trip, arm-to-arm inoculations could be made once the expedition reached America. Following what must have been a tortuous and monotonous course, this famous expedition passed through the Antilles, Mexico, Central America, New Granada, Venezuela, Peru, the viceroyalty of Buenos Aires, and came at last to Chile in the first days of January, 1808.[28] Nearly a thousand persons were sometimes vaccinated in a week.

Moved by the tragedy of the epidemic in 1797, Mexico welcomed the first smallpox virus delivered in the viceroyalty in 1804 by Thomas Murphy. Some believe, however, that Dr. Juan de Arboleya brought the first lymph from Havana in 1804, at the command of Viceroy Iturrigaray. The significance of the delivery was vouchsafed in the initial vaccination—that of a small son of the viceroy at the hands of Arboleya.[29] A Mexican commission, composed of the most distinguished medical men in the realm,[30] was appointed to perpetuate the virus.

Before smallpox virus had been distributed in

[27] Circular of José Antonio Caballero, San Ildefonso, 1 September, 1802. The agreement was signed by Balmis in Madrid, 24 August, 1803.

[28] Vicuña Mackenna, *op. cit.*, pp. 199-200.

[29] Alexander von Humboldt, cited in Flores, *op. cit.*, II, 218.

[30] Don José Joaquín Pina, Don Manuel Vasconcelos, Don Mariano Cardoso, Drs. Luis Montaña, Don Vicente Ferrer. Flores, *op. cit.*, II, 218.

America, the Spanish government had already adopted the practice of disseminating by royal circular a description of any remedy which stood the slightest empirical test. In the last of the eighteenth century[31] a tropical disease induced by jigger fleas, which burrow under the nails causing pain and infection, was supposed to have been routed by the circulation in 1786 of a document prescribing the application of raw olive oil to kill both the insect and the pus sac. In 1793 copies of a prescription for rheumatic pains and venereal and scorbutic diseases, which had been practiced with success in New Orleans, were circulated in America.[32] In 1795 a royal order required that the navel of infants should be anointed with balsam of copaiba[33] as soon as the umbilical cord was cut to prevent a species of epilepsy (tetanus) which had raised the infant mortality, especially in Cuba, to frightful figures.

A growing feeling of humanitarianism and of state responsibility in public health was vouchsafed in a pamphlet espousing—in conformity with Catholic doctrine—the cause of unborn children.[34]

[31] November 20, 1786.

[32] Real cédula de 22 de Julio de 1793. Fuenzalida, *op. cit.*, pp. 136-137.

[33] In Lima the remedy became the subject of the bachelor's thesis of José Manuel Valdés. *Concertatio medica de balsami copaibae in infantvm convvlsionibvs praestantissimo vsv, quam pro gradv baccalavreatvs obtinendo, avspice deo et ivbente dilectissimo Carolo IV, svstinebit Joseph Emmanuel Valdes chirvrgvs phisic. baccal. praeside D. D. Hipolyto Vnanve anatomes professore.* In Reg. Ac. Pontif. Divi Marci Academia. Die Febrvarii Anni MDCCCVII.

[34] Francisco González Laguna, *El zelo sacerdotal para con los niños no nacidos.* Lima, 1781.

In the latter half of the eighteenth century interest in obstetrics grew rapidly. It was natural, consequently, that Caesarean operations should be performed contemporaneously with the experimental study of anatomy and in response to the suffering and mortalities of childbirth. In 1772, Dr. José Manuel Rodríguez published a book[35] promoting the Caesarean which had the happy result of influencing Viceroy Bucareli to issue an order that this operation should be performed under pain of drastic punishment. It was on December 18, 1794, that such an operation was performed by Anthony Terry in Tucumán with the approval and upon the orders of the *alcalde mayor*, Pedro Gregorio López. Although the infant survived only fifteen minutes, the doctors believed it would have lived longer had the family permitted the operation earlier.[36] Two years later the operation under certain conditions was made compulsory in America and the Philippines. True to the paternalistic tradition, the instructions were so minute as to describe the instrument to be used and to specify exactly how and where it should be inserted, especially in an operation after the death of the woman.[37]

So spectacular were the medical discoveries in the

[35] *La caridad del sacerdote para con los niños encerrados en el vientre de sus madres difuntas y documentos de la utilidad y necesidad de su práctica.* México, 1772.

[36] *Mercurio Peruano*, Lima, 1794, as cited in Valdizán, *op. cit.*, I, 170. It has not been possible to verify Valdizán's citation with the Fuentes edition of the *Mercurio.*

[37] Real cédula dada en Aranjuez, 13 de Abril de 1804, announced in Lima, 4 March, 1805. The document is transcribed in Valdizán, *op. cit.*, III, 11-14.

last half of the eighteenth century that credulity was built up not only for experiment but for sham discoveries. The imagination was leaping so far and so daringly that it was suggested, in anticipation of the present-day use of "rays" in medicine, and in the very cloisters of the university, that electricity should be converted to the art of healing.[38]

But others of these wild hopes and imaginings could end in naught but frustration and disappointment. One Peruvian doctor, Baltázar Villalobos, pretended to have discovered in 1804 a revolutionary cure for leprosy, although little evidence beyond his own testimony remains[39] concerning this mysterious remedy, which was probably little more than a variation of pomatum. An index to the excitement caused by this claim can be found in Viceroy Marqués de Avilés' agreement to provide public facilities for the treatment of the disease.

Wilder still was the dream of that modern spirit, Dr. José Flores, to use the amphibious lizards or

[38] AGG, A1., 3-12, 12813, 1928; *Propositiones de rebus naturalibus defendendae a D. Josepho Cecilio del Valle . . .*, Guatemalae, M.DCC.XCIV. Unde Francklin o fulgurum minis sedificia liberavit ope cuspidum, vulgo *para-rayo* . . . . Quod attinet ad aeconomiam animalem & vegetationem plantarum, contra easque affectiones vim maximam habet, quae contractiones, paralysis, suppressionis, aliisque id genus titulis donantur.

Ibid., *Theses ex universa philosophia quas D. Joannes Ferminus de Ayzinena et Piñol . . .*, 21 Julii Anni D. M. D. CCCVI.: . . . tali absdubio principio ducti plures phisici, tentarunt vi electrica curare morbos, experientia ipsa magis ac magis eos impellente. . . . Igitur Turrius experimentis electricismi ab ipsomet institutis binos homines curandos suscepit. . . .

[39] Carlos A. Romero (ed.), *Memoria del virrey del Perú, Marqués de Avilés*, p. 22; Valdizán, *op. cit.*, III, 51-59.

newts of Amatitán in Guatemala for the cure of cancer. In Italy the journals published the remedy, and a special Italian edition of Flores' work was issued. Although some unsuccessful experiments were performed there, where cancer was supposed to be bad, Italian criticism was dismissed on the grounds that the venal Italians would have been more laudatory had they been paid and the work produced in France.[40] The experiments were pursued in Mexico, Cádiz, Málaga, and in France "with success," but it was discovered that whereas five or six lizards sufficed in Guatemala it required thirty in Europe to produce the necessary "perspiration, . . . slavering, . . . and copious evacuations of the bladder and bowels."

An especially acrimonious controversy among the medical, and even non-medical, men resulted in Mexico. Dr. Antonio León Gama on the one hand and Manuel Antonio Moreno and Alejo Ramón Sánchez on the other battled over whether or not the remedy should be considered a "specific" on the basis of haphazard reports of Dr. Flores' works by unqualified, ignorant persons. Before the end of the year 1782 this exotic prescription was recommended for rabies, leprosy, St. Anthony's disease, King's evil, cancer, buboes, all kinds of consumption, intermittent fevers, hypochondria, gout, and hysteria![41] It was a

[40] Biblioteca Nacional de Guatemala, *Discursos,* I, No. 41, MSS., "Roma 2 dic^re de 178 [torn]."

[41] Most of the literature of this controversy has been collected (Biblioteca Nacional de Guatemala, *Discursos,* I) and, judging from the internal evidence, the tracts made their appearance in approximately this order:

Especifico nuevamente descubierto en el Reyno de Goatemala,

sign of the time that the sponsor of this remedy thought fit to masquerade as a "patriotic spirit" and that the reaction of a large faction was scientific.

The newts of Guatemala were almost matched by the "martial pills" or iron of Mexico. In 1774 all intellectual Mexico was bestirred when there appeared a poster announcing the appearance of Gaicinto Gibelli's treatise on the use of iron in the cure of many diseases.[42] The author of the poster was sanguine enough to declare the concoction a remedy for lack of appetite, dropsy, sour stomach, belly ache, chronic diarrhea, white flux with blood, "stubborn intermittent fevers," gout and rheumatism, scurvy,

---

para la curacion radical del horrible mal del cancro, y otros mas frecuentes (experimentado ya favorablemente en esta Capital de México). Su avtor El Dr. José Flores del Gremio, y Claustro de la Real Universidad de dicha Goatemala, su Patria. Dase al publico a expensas de un espiritu patriotico. Reimpreso con las licencias necesarias. Mexico, 1782.

Reflexiones sobre el uso de las Lagartijas [que escribieron el Lic. D. Manuel Antonio Moreno v el Br. Alejo Ramón Sánchez]. Mexico, 1782.

Antonio León Gama, *Disertacion sobre el uso medicinal de las lagartijas de Guatemala.* Mexico, 1782.

Discurso Critico que sobre el uso de las Lagartijas como especifico contra muchas enfermedades, produjo D. Joseph Vicente Garcia de la Vega, Profesor de Medicina en la Imperial Corte de Mexico. Mexico, 1782.

Carta apologetica de las reflexiones sobre el uso de las lagartijas que escribieron el Lic. D. Manuel Moreno y el Br. Alejo Ramon Sanchez. Mexico, 1782.

Respuesta satisfactoria a la carta apologetica, que escribieron el Lic D. Manuel Antonio Moreno y el Br. D. Alejo Ramos Sanchez de algunas proposiciones contenidas en la Instruccion sobre el remedio de las Lagartijas, que escribio D. Antonio de Leon y Gama. Mexico, 1783.

[42] *Due dissertazioni sopra li ventaggi, che si ottengono in medicina dall' uso del ferro . . . .* Genova, 1767.

hypochondria, "paleness and wasting away." Dr. José Ignacio Bartolache, leading professor of medicine, and among the most critical Mexicans of his generation, as Dr. Flores was of his in Guatemala, sought to solve the secret of Gibelli's formula. He became convinced of its efficacy in a limited number of diseases. Iron, so destructive in swords and cannons, was about to compensate for its injuries to mankind! The rector of the University of Mexico provided the *Salón General de Actos* in which Dr. Bartolache, on July 28, 29, and 30, 1774, defended the product against all objections and doubts with "great courtesy and seriousness."[43] The *Tribunal del Protomedicato* made no objections and posters were printed and distributed in Aztec on the use of Gibelli's martial pills *(Pastillas Marciales Gibellinas)*.[44]

II

The epoch of Dr. Flores and Dr. Bartolache was a sad one in science, for with the willingness to experiment and to accept the new there did not come a corresponding mastery. The sum of the full but weakly fledged young doctor's knowledge in the seventeenth century embraced a broken mosaic of the *Aphorisms*, the *Prognostics*, and the *Ratione Victus* of Hippocrates. These, together with the *Differentiis febrium* and *De crisibus* of Galen, continued to be

[43] AGN, *Libro de Gobierno, desde 1771 hasta 1774, XXI: Noticia plausible para sanos y enfermos.*

[44] *Ibid., Netemachtiliztli. Lu Itechpa in ce tancuican pahtli, inic in Macehualtin quimatizque yeiman, quenin, ihuan quezqui quicelizque.*

basic in medical science until near the close of the eighteenth century.[45] The student, therefore, knew no anatomical study beyond that which Galen, dissecting a few monkeys, had written in Alexandria nearly sixteen hundred years before.[46] However, in Mexico change in texts was possible, for during a great part of the colonial period (from 1668) texts were not named in the constitutions of the university but were designated by the rector and a junta of professors.[47]

The precepts of Avicenna (979-1037), as the most respected of the Arabic physicians, engaged their attention, but the work of the infidel ultimately encountered official displeasure and was dropped from the lists of texts in Mexico in 1778[48] for a more com-

[45] At the time of the Palafox y Mendoza's revisal of the statutes of the University of Mexico the first year was devoted to: *De elementis, De temperamentis, De humoribus, De anatomicis administrationibus, De facultatibus, De pulsibus et urinis;* the second year: *De differentiis febrium, Ad Glauconem de medendi methodo, De sanguinis misione* [Galen]; the third: *Aphorismorum* [Quo et quando oportet purgari], . . . *Rhazis al Almansorem;* fourth year: *De crisibus, De diebus decretoriis, Methodi mendendi* [Galen].

[46] *De anatomicis administrationibus.*

[47] Boerhaave was so thoroughly in vogue in Mexico around 1771 as to be called "the immortal." AGN, *Libro de Gobierno, desde 1771 hasta 1774, Positiones ex universa medicina theoretica dipromatae* . . . [Thesis of José Paredes]: Ad eas porro disserte, ac eleganter evolvendas Immortalis Boerhavii cedro atque cupresso perdignam Pathologiam defensabo. *Instit. Med.* 695. In this treatise Paredes referred to J. de Gorter, Lorenzo Bellini, Frederick Hoffman, and maintained that the body of man, in a healthy condition, could be shown by reason and experiment to function naturally through certain stable laws of chemistry, physics, and mechanics.

[48] AGN, *Libros de la Universidad de México: De Medicina . . . Aforismos de Hippocrates, prognosticos, epidemias* (tres asignaciones de puntos).

plete return to Hippocrates—a return considered, according to Gilbert Murray, a progressive step in the eighteenth century. The gap was partially filled by an order of Charles III that the study of medicine should be essayed through the *Instituciones médicas* of the Spanish doctor Andrés Piquer.[49] And sometimes to these were added the ideas and texts of Rhazis (850-c.932 [al Almanzorem]) who represented observation of the patient and a general discrediting of the Galeno-Hippocratic school, and Guido Guido (d.1569), organizer of the medical faculty of the Collège de France, and especially of "the immortal" Dutch physician, Hermann Boerhaave. Although Hippocrates and Avicenna continued to dominate in Lima, new authors were established here and there in America. Points for medical examinations in the University of Santo Domingo were taken from the writings of Martín Martínez (1684-1734), the Spanish "eagle of science" dedicated to the study of physics and chemistry,[50] while in the University of Quito the text of Boerhaave and the commentaries of Albert von Haller (1708-1777), Swiss anatomist and physiologist, consumed the first two years. None the less, the third year was absorbed in a study of "the divine" Valles and Piquer. In the fourth the text of Lorenzo Heister (1683-1758), German anatomist and antagonist of Linnaeus, held sway. Bishop Joseph Pérez Calama, of Quito, in offering a modernized univer-

[49] Real cédula de abril de 1778.

[50] Max Henríquez Ureña, *op. cit.*, p. 91.

sity curriculum in 1791, signified only one text in the study of medicine, Francisco Solano de Luque ("*el Pulsita*," 1648-1778), *Idioma de la Naturaleza*.[51]

The reform movements in medical education near the end of the eighteenth century revolutionized the literature of what gradually gained the dignity of medical science. An examination of the changes which took place in Guatemala, Peru, and Mexico will illustrate the development. Under such men as José Flores and Narciso Esparragoza in Guatemala aspirants began to make use of a variety of treatises. One student (1803-1804) referred to François Quesnay (1694-1774) on inflammation and gangrene, Benjamin Bell (1746-1806), conventional Edinburgh authority, on tumors and ulcers, Felix Fontana (1730-1805), Italian physiologist, on wounds and poison complications, Pierre Lassus (1741-1807), French authority on typhus and typhoid, and others on surgical methods, and Percival Pott (1713-1788), Irish author of a work on contusions, on dislocations and fractures.[52] Luis Franco offered to defend his theses in surgery "in accordance with the doctrines of accredited authors, principally those of the publications of the Royal Academy of Surgery and Medicine in Paris."[53] And not long afterwards another student sustained his tenets not only with

[51] *Plan de Estudios*, 1 vol., 3 parts, Quito, 1791-1792.

[52] AGG, A1., 3-12, 12826, 1933. *Medicina Operatoria, examen de Pedro Molina*, 1803 or 1804.

[53] AGG, A1., 3-12, 12819, 1930, theses of Luis Franco and Mariano Antonio de Larrave, 28 March, 1798.

reference to "the pulsist," Francisco Solano de Luque (1684-1738), but also depended upon the distinguished experimentalist, David McBride (1726-1778), the naturalist, George Louis Leclerc, count of Buffon (1707-1790), and the clinician, William Cullen (1710-1790).[54] The range of medical books cited in the inedited medical works of Dr. Narciso Esparragoza in Guatemala is indeed surprising.[55] The new material was so abundant and oppressive that Dr. Esparragoza was the only man in Guatemala considered to have dominated it. He was prevailed upon to give a free course on the subject in the university,[56] in which he roamed at large among the authorities of the world. An inventory of the books and instruments of a *protomédico* of Guatemala dated 1776, includes such works as those of Jenner, Thomas Burnet, Richard Morton, Thomas Sydenham, Boerhaave, Isbrandde Diemerbroeck, Francisco Solano de Luque, Martín Martínez, N. Cevola Lemeri,[57] Robert Boyle, Oswaldo Crolii,[58] a treatise on electricity, and two microscopes.[59]

[54] *Ibid.*, 12827, 1933, thesis of Mariano Viscarra, 14 January, 1804.

[55] Biblioteca Nacional de Guatemala, manuscript texts of Mariano Zenteno: (1) Lección de Huesos, (2) de Músculos, (3) de Visceras, (4) de nervios, arterias, y venas, (5) de sentidos.

[56] Biblioteca Nacional de Guatemala. MSS. de *Curso Theorico-Practico de Operaciones de Cirugia.* Lo dictó gratis el Dr. Dn. Narciso Esparragoza y Gallardo, Cirujano de camara de honor.

[57] *Curso chimico.*

[58] *Basilica chimica.*

[59] Archivo Colonial de Guatemala, 246-8: Inventario y avaluos de los bienes que quedaron por muerte del Doctor Don Manuel Davalos y Porras, protomedico de este reino, y catedratico de prima de medicina, Año de 1776.

It soon becomes obvious that the bases of progress were being laid during a whole century in which the medical curriculum remained relatively static. The modernization of medical instruction in Peru might well date from the professional arrival of the celebrated Hipólito Unánue. It was in the *Hospital de San Andrés* in Lima that Unánue passed the gantlet of the bachelor's and licenciate's degrees to become a doctor (1783). Thereafter, all theses emanating from San Marcos de Lima always touched mathematical, physical, and natural topics with a fundamental respect. To the question, put in one of the routine literary exercises which spread the fame of this bright student, "Will medicine prove more useful and illustrious when accompanied by *belles-lettres* and the exact sciences?" Unánue answered affirmatively with such convincing knowledge and enchanting language that he was raised to the secretaryship of the progressive *Amantes del País.* His appointment as professor of anatomy was followed only three years later, in 1792, with the inauguration of an anatomical amphitheatre. His zeal was that of a pioneer, for in the inaugural address of the anatomical amphitheatre, he spoke on "The Decadence and Restoration of Peru." The oration, as already noted, contained a denunciation of the deplorable state of medicine and the lamentable and tragic state of public health.

By 1795 the Royal Amphitheatre had become the center of a group of fifty physicians, some of them trained in the most advanced institutions of Europe, who were to constitute the supporting nucleus for the establishment of a separate medical college. This school, the Royal College of Medicine and Surgery of San Fernando, was the reward of the passion of Unánue and the medical faction for science and health. Sanctioned in 1808, the institution was transferred from the University of San Marcos, inaugurated on October 1, 1811, and confirmed by Royal *cédula,* May 9, 1815. And in the same year Viceroy Abascal, on behalf of Unánue, petitioned the crown for the creation of a chair of chemistry, physics, medical institutions, *materia medica,* botany, surgery, obstetrics, and pharmacy. From the stars to pharmacy and obstetrics was a long distance, but not so great as to abash Unánue and a small coterie of medical doctors in Lima.[60]

Like most Latin-American scholars of the period, this eminent Peruvian's tastes were catholic enough to embrace a fundamental knowledge of auxiliary sciences. He became the author of a series of guides or handbooks[61] which had their culmination in one of the most important scientific works produced in the New World during the colonial period—his *Observaciones sobre el Clima de Lima.*[62] So profound was the influence exercised by Unánue upon the mind of Peruvian youth that the "medical faction" finally

[60] Valdizán, *op. cit.*, II, 13-14, 24-26, 65-124, III, 105-106; Archivo del Colegio de Medicina y Cirugía, *Libro de Matrículas de 1808 a 1817;* B. Vicuña Mackenna, *La revolución de la independencia del Perú* (Lima, 1860), pp. 108-109.

[61] *Guía política eclesiástica y militar del Virreinato del Perú.* Lima, 1793-1797.

[62] 2 vols., Madrid, 1815.

came to be synonymous with revolution not only in science but in politics.

Unfortunately, the growth of medical schools in Mexico did not involve the whole-hearted acceptance of modern technique as in Peru. The cause lies in the early rise of these Mexican schools, the multiplicity of which prevented anyone from becoming distinguished. Through the solicitude of Dr. José Mercado the *Academia de Medicina* was established in 1735 and approved by the king. The attempts of the academy, however, to promote a college of medicine were regarded as in competition with the university and defeated by the cloister. In imitation of the example of Cádiz and Barcelona the Mexicans established a School of Surgery *(Escuela de Cirugía)* in Mexico City in 1768,[63] and unofficially installed it in 1770 against the complaints of the *protomedicato* that such a school would require the importation of Spaniards, since the Mexicans were not competent, and would result in a plague of Romance surgeons. The new school of surgery professed to follow the practices of similar institutions in the peninsula.[64] In the *Hospital de Jesús* there existed by 1775 an academy of practical medicine called *Academia Proregia Mariana de Jesús Nazareno* which was still in ex-

[63] By a royal decree dated 16 March, 1768, the school was provided with a chair of "practical anatomy." Due to the projection of a more thorough study of medical education in Mexico, medicine there is not treated with proportional emphasis in this chapter.

[64] Under the inspection of the *protomedicato* until 1804, it could boast chairs of anatomy, physiology, operations (theoretical), and clinical surgery (practical).

istence when Morelos was executed. The drift of the times was indicated in another institution, the *Academia Médica-Físico-Botánica-Farmacéutica* operated near the end of the eighteenth century.[65] As one of the features of the academic reforms, a professor of the University of Mexico had become a dissector of human bodies in the Botanical Garden.[66] But these many schools and chairs brought enervating duplication.[67] Dr. Luis Montaña, arch conservative in politics, overthrew Hippocrates and introduced the study of chemistry and pharmacy into the viceroyalty before independence.

Medical progress was achieved, with the disintegration of the old methods and institutions, at the rather dangerous price of anarchy—anarchy accentuated by the war of Mexican independence. But the war itself, as was natural,[68] in some respects proved a boon to medicine. Although the University was suspended with the quartering of troops in its building, medical societies sprang up. One worthy of mention, the *Academia de Medicina Práctica de México*, became the most distinguished as a promoter

[65] Flores, *op. cit.*, pp. 145-165, 265.

[66] AGN, *Libro de Claustros, desde 1779 hasta 1788*, claustro de 14 abril de 1786.

[67] Dr. Antonio Serrano, professor of surgery in the Royal School of Surgery to José Mesía, "Oydor de esta Rl. Audiencia y Juez Protector del Hospital Rl. de Naturales," 15 April, 1815. AGN, *Libro de Gobierno, desde 1813 hasta 1821*.

[68] Flores, *op. cit.*, II, 145, says that he found in the archives of the Royal School of Surgery a copy of *Arte de hacer las relaciones médico-quimico-legales* by Licenciate Magín Camí, surgeon of the royal armies.

of clinical subjects, especially pathology and pathological anatomy.

Even from so short a treatment as this it is possible to see how much remains to be done and how many lessons to be learned or relearned on the subject of Hispanic colonial medical culture. Knowledge on the whole subject has not reached the stage of the monograph, not to mention that of the synthesis. On an institution so arresting and so important as the *protomedicato* the first treatise remains to be written. From the scanty survey presented, however, it can be seen that the blythe denunciations of extreme medical retardation in the viceroyalties are as unfounded as those on education and philosophy and with just as little consideration for the relative advancement of Europe and English America. The evidence is sufficient to indicate that any man who ventures to appraise cultural progress in Latin America should diligently investigate the sources before dismissing it as three hundred years behind the rest of the world.

Index

www.ingramcontent.com/pod-product-compliance
Lightning Source LLC
LaVergne TN
LVHW091638100826
845152LV00005B/85
* 9 7 8 1 6 2 8 2 0 1 2 1 5 *